Grammar

Games and Activities

New Edition

Peter Watcyn-Jones
and
Deirdre Howard-Williams

To Polly, Philippa and other teachers I have met whose kind comments make me want to go on writing books

P W-J

And to all who love language and how it works

D H-W

Series Editor
Peter Watcyn-Jones

PENGUIN ENGLISH

Pearson Education Limited
Edinburgh Gate
Harlow
Essex CM20 2JE, England
and Associated Companies throughout the world.

ISBN 978-0-582-46563-3

First published 1995
This edition published 2001

Ninth impression 2009

Design and typesetting by Ferdinand Pageworks, London
Illustrations by Rupert Besley, Mark Davis, Bruce Hogarth, Jean de Lemos and Ross Thomson
Printed in China   SWTC/09

Published by Pearson Education Limited in association with Penguin Books Ltd, both
companies being subsidiaries of Pearson plc.

For a complete list of the titles available from Penguin English please write to your local
Pearson Education office or to: Penguin English Marketing Department,
Pearson Education, Edinburgh Gate, Harlow, Essex CM20 2JE.

Contents

Key to contents table

Activity type		Preparation	
🧍	individual	📄	1 handout to copy
🧍🧍	pair work	📄	several handouts to copy
🧍🧍🧍	group work	✂️	1 handout to copy and cut up
🧍🧍🧍🧍	whole class activity	✂️	several handouts to copy and cut up
🎓	teacher-led activity	✂️	handout to be cut up into several pieces or into cards

Game/Activity	Time	Grammar/Topic	Activity type	Preparation	Pages
Elementary/Pre-Intermediate					
13 Do you know me well?	20–25 mins	Present simple, asking and answering questions using auxiliaries			6/57
14 Can you follow instructions?	15 mins	Imperatives to follow instructions			7/58
15 Make a sentence – score a point!	10 mins per game	Past tense of irregular verbs			7/59–61
16 I like this but I don't like that!	20 mins	Expressing likes and dislikes followed by a noun or gerund			8/62–63
17 A family tree	15–20 mins	Present simple; use of indefinite article with jobs; possessive 's			9/64
18 Left, right, up, down	20 mins	Prepositions; imperatives to give instructions			9/65–67
19 True or false?	20 mins	Asking questions in various tenses; using determiners			10/68
20 Find the differences	15–20 mins	Present continuous; *There is/are*; prepositions of place			10/69–70
21 What did you do last week?	20 mins	Past simple			11/71–72
22 Do you have have a good memory?	15 mins	Present simple; *There is/are*; prepositions of place			11/73
23 Biographies	20–25 mins	Past simple; asking *WH-* questions; time indicators; spelling			12/74–75
24 Life style surveys	30 mins	Asking questions in present simple; frequency adverbs; using determiners			13/76–77
Pre-Intermediate/Intermediate					
25 Find someone who …	25 mins	Present perfect and past simple			14/78
26 Conjunctions bingo	15 mins per game	Conjunctions of time; other conjunctions			14/79–80
27 Where are the carrots?	15–20 mins	Prepositions of place; present simple			15/81
28 Four people's diaries	20 mins	Present continuous with future meaning			16/82–83
29 Trace the route	15 mins	Giving directions using imperatives; using adverbs and prepositions			16/84–85
30 Group opinions	25 mins	Tag questions; expression of number and amount			17/86

iv

v

Introduction

Grammar Games and Activities 1 forms part of the Penguin series of resource books for teachers. This edition has been thoroughly revised and updated to provide teachers with 60 activities for practising and revising grammar. These activities range in level from elementary to advanced and include a wide variety of types: information gap, jigsaw reading, surveys, bingo, questionnaires, giving and following instructions, asking and answering questions, find the differences, etc.

Each activity contains material to be photocopied, usually one or two sheets, and clear step-by-step instructions to the teacher on preparation and organisation. **Grammar Games and Activities 1** can be used with adults and teenagers at all levels and in different classes to give extra practice in grammar in a fun and stimulating way.

The grammar items in the book have been carefully chosen to cover a wide base with the emphasis on the most frequently encountered e.g. asking and answering questions in various tenses. Each activity is centred on one specific grammar point which is clearly explained with examples in the Teacher's Notes and most will additionally practise supplementary grammar points, which are also presented in detail.

Most of the activities will involve the students working in pairs or in small groups, which is an excellent way of making the learning process more dynamic and enjoyable. Students will see that grammar is a necessary part of communication and can be fun!

The majority of the ideas in this book are based on ideas which have been tried and tested, particularly while teaching in Scandinavia. Where someone else's idea has been consciously used, this is of course acknowledged. If anyone feels they can lay prior claim to any of the other activities, acknowledgement will gladly be made in future editions of this book.

The organisation of this book

Grammar Games and Activities 1 has been organised by level. There are five levels:

1 Beginner/Elementary
2 Elementary/Pre-intermediate
3 Pre-intermediate/Intermediate
4 Intermediate/Upper Intermediate
5 Upper Intermediate/Advanced

with twelve activities in each level.

However, classes vary enormously and these levels are only a guide, since the games in this book practise and reinforce vital grammar items which can be useful to everyone.

Classroom organisation

The activities in **Grammar Games and Activities 1** are sufficiently flexible to be done in classes of all sizes and extra suggestions are made for very large numbers.

Grammar point

The detailed contents list will show at a glance the grammar point that is being practised in each game so this is the first place to look if you wish to find a game to either present or revise a specific grammar point with your class.

Some grammar points are dealt with in several different games so you can go back to the book a few lessons later and find another activity to use for reinforcement.

Time

There is an indication in the contents list and also in the Teacher's Notes as to the approximate time each activity will take. This will of course vary from class to class and will depend on how thoroughly you wish to exploit the activity. However, it does give an indication and can help you decide if you wish to make the game the main focus of the lesson or use it either at the beginning (as an ice-breaker and introduction) or at the end of the lesson (as a relaxation and revision).

Preparing the activity before class

The Teacher's Notes to each activity have a special section: Preparation. This section tells you exactly what you need to do before the class starts i.e., how many pages to photocopy, how many copies are needed and if the copies need to be cut up in any way.

Introducing the activity

The Teacher's Notes start with suggestions on how to introduce each activity. It may often be useful to revise the grammar point first and write some examples up for students to refer to while the game is going on. These can be wiped off once the game has got started and students start to use the structures automatically.

Always explain very clearly what to do and it is often a good idea to do an example yourself with one of the students.

For most of the activities it is a good idea to set a time-limit and write this up so that everyone can see it. Give a warning shortly before it expires so that students can start to finish off. It may be that some students have not finished but it is inevitable that people will finish at different times and it may be a better idea to play the game a second time.

Pair work and group work

There are various types of activities: some where students work individually, some where they work in pairs and some where they cooperate in small groups.

Where possible, rearrange the classroom slightly to make it easier for students to work in pairs or groups without disturbing others. Where this is not possible, students doing pair work should work with the person sitting beside them or the person in front or behind (they just need to turn round). For group work, two students can easily turn their chairs round to face two others behind them. When you have an uneven number of students, most pair activities can be done by three people (if necessary, two students against one).

As far as possible, vary the pairs and groups so that students do not always work with the same people. It can sometimes be useful to mix stronger and weaker students in a small group so that they can help one another.

The enormous advantage of working in pairs and groups is that it gives everyone a chance to speak in a non-threatening environment, i.e. with a fellow-student and not in front of the teacher and the whole class. Students will learn from each other in a natural way that approximates more to the world outside and gets away from some of the constraints of the classroom. If this type of activity is new to them, it is useful to explain its advantages and to encourage them to take full advantage by participating as much as they can and sticking strictly to English!

The role of the teacher while this is going on is to facilitate communication by walking round the classroom, pausing briefly beside each pair/group. If all is going well, just encourage and move on. If things are not going so well, offer help and encouragement as needed to get students working well together.

While walking round, it is useful to have a small notebook or piece of paper on which you note down any persistent mistakes you hear or common problems. You can discuss these with the whole class during the feedback session – it is usually better to avoid saying who made each mistake as this can have a discouraging effect!

Feedback session and follow-up work

Each activity should end with a feedback session for the whole class.

The Teacher's Notes contain detailed suggestions on how to conduct this session for each individual activity. This checking and evaluation is an integral part of the activity and it is important to leave enough time for it.

Teachers may like to extend the activity into some kind of written follow-up work to reinforce what has been practised in class and most of the games have ideas for further activities and for homework.

A note about photocopying

Since this is a photocopiable book with each activity containing one or more handouts, it may be worth looking at ways of reducing the costs – both in terms of time and money. The material to be photocpied can be divided into two types: (a) handouts which the students write on, and (b) material which the students use but do not write on. Of the latter, many are cut into cards.

For materials that can be re-used, wherever possible try mounting them on cards and protecting them either by laminating them or (a cheaper solution) by keeping them in clear plastic folders. The extra initial effort will certainly pay off as subsequent photocopying costs and time will be greatly reduced.

Part 1: **Teacher's notes**

Beginner/Elementary

1   Find someone who ...

Time: 20 minutes
Type of activity: Whole class mingle, asking and
                         answering questions
Preparation: Make one copy of page 37
                         per student

Grammar points
Asking questions in the present simple tense
Do you ...?
Short answers
Yes, I do./No, I don't.
Asking longer *WH-* questions
What do you ...; Who do you ...;
Who is ...; Where does ...
Answering longer questions with simple
information
It's .../I'm .../They're ...

Method

1   Give each student a copy of the handout.

2   Give them time to read through the
    questions and ask you anything they do
    not understand.

3   Students then stand up and walk round
    the room, trying to find someone who fits
    each of the descriptions on their sheet.
    They start by asking the question and if
    they get a *Yes* answer, they follow up with
    a second question to get more information.
    Then they note down the person's name
    and the information on their sheet.

4   If they get a *No* answer, they ask another
    question and continue asking the same
    person questions until they get a *Yes*. Once
    they have noted down any information,
    they should move on and ask somebody
    else. This is to ensure that students talk to
    as many different people as possible.

5   Stop the activity when most students have
    completed their sheets and have a whole
    class feedback. You could go through all
    the descriptions orally and see whose name
    came up the most.

6   This could lead on to written homework
    where students write a few sentences about
    what they have found out about others in
    the group.

2   Bingo: What's the time?

Time: 10 minutes per game
Type of activity: Teacher-led with students working
                         individually (or in pairs in larger
                         classes)
Preparation: Make one copy of page 38. Leave
                         the Teacher's board as it is, but cut
                         up the Teacher's numbers into 24
                         squares.

                         Copy the students' cards on pages
                         39 and 40 and cut them out – one
                         card per student or one per pair if
                         the class is very large. If you plan to
                         play the game twice, give each
                         student two cards to start.

Grammar point
Telling the time
It's ... o'clock/past/to/quarter/half, etc.

Method

1   Give out the Bingo cards. Allow students a
    few minutes to look through the times
    they have before you start. You might like
    to do a quick revision of how times are
    expressed.

2   Put the 24 squares you have cut up into
    some kind of container and draw them out
    one at a time. Say the time on the square
    and place it on your board. If the students
    have a clock on their cards that shows that
    time, they cross it out.

3   Continue until a student has crossed out
    every clock, at which point they shout out
    'Bingo!'

4   Now stop the game and ask the student to
    say the time on each clock s/he has crossed
    out. Check on your board that these times
    have been called out.

5   If a mistake has been made, continue with
    the game until somebody has won.

6   You can then play again with different
    cards for further revision. This time it
    might be a good idea to walk round the
    classroom with the squares in the
    container, asking individual students to
    pick one out and read out the time to the
    rest of the class.

3 Bingo: Telephone numbers

Time: 10 minutes per game
Type of activity: Teacher-led with students working individually (or in pairs for larger classes)
Preparation: Make one copy of page 41. Keep the Teacher's board as it is and cut up the Teacher's numbers to make 24 squares.

Copy the Student's cards on pages 42 and 43 and cut them out – one card for each student or one per pair for larger classes. If you plan to play the game twice, make two cards per student.

Grammar point
Practising how telephone numbers are said
each number said separately; double two; oh

Method

1 As Activity 2. Revise how to say telephone numbers first if necessary.

2 Repeat with a second card for further practice and this time invite students to pick out a square and read out the number.

3 You might like to extend the activity by asking students to read out real phone numbers e.g., their own, numbers of local services, hotels, etc. and discussing how to phone locally, nationally or internationally.

There are few activities that can beat Bingo for concentration and intensive listening practice!

4 What's my uncle's job?

Time: 20–30 minutes, depending on how many jobs you use
Type of activity: Whole class activity for a small class (up to 15)
Group work for larger classes
Preparation: Make a copy of the handout on page 44 and cut out the cards. For classes larger than 15, make two copies.

Grammar points
Asking questions (third person singular)
Does he work indoors/outdoors/alone/in a team/in a

shop? etc. *Does he use a computer/his hands? etc. Is he a ...?*
Short *Yes/No* answers with adverbs of frequency
Yes, always/usually/often/sometimes.
No, never/hardly ever/not usually.

Method

1 First practise with the whole class the type of questions to be asked. Tell them you have an uncle and they are going to find out what your uncle's job is by asking you questions. You can only answer *Yes* or *No* with an adverb and they only have ten questions before they must guess.

2 Imagine your uncle is a film star (but do not say this). As the class ask you questions, answer with *Yes* or *No* and an adverb of frequency. You may like to write the seven possible adverbs on the board for reference (see grammar point above). If necessary, also write up some suggestions for questions. (These can be rubbed off once the game gets under way and the students become more confident.)

3 When they have guessed your uncle's job, ask for a volunteer to come up and pick one of the jobs you have cut up. The class then ask questions to try to guess.

4 Variations: divide the class into two teams. One team provides a person to come up, take a job and answer. The other team have to try and guess within ten guesses. Award points for correct guesses.

5 For a large class (more than 15) divide the class into groups (3–5 students) and give everyone in the group two jobs. They are then questioned by the other members of their group. In this case, keep two or three jobs back to do with the whole class at the end as a round-up.

5 What are the missing numbers?

Time: 10–15 minutes
Type of activity: Information gap with students working in pairs
Preparation: Make one copy of the handout on page 45 per pair of students and cut it into two.

Grammar point
Cardinal numbers
nought to over a thousand

Method

1   Practise numbers and the pronunciation of letters of the alphabet (A–F) first if you feel this is necessary.

2   Divide the class into pairs (A and B) and give each student a copy of the appropriate handout.

3   Students sit facing each other, but make sure that their handout is hidden from their partner.

4   Explain that they each have twelve numbers on their cards and twelve spaces. By asking their partner the question: *What's the number in square (e.g.1A)?* they will both be able to fill in and complete their cards as between them they have all the information.

5   When everyone is ready and understands what to do, set a time-limit (e.g. five minutes). Everyone starts together and must stop at the end of the time given, whether they have finished or not.

6   Stop everyone when time is up and let them compare their handouts to see how well they did.

7   Do a quick class feedback by asking students to tell you which numbers go in which squares.

6   Fill in the missing dates

Time: 10–15 minutes
Type of activity: Information gap with students working in pairs
Preparation: Make one copy of the handout on page 46 per pair of students and cut it into two

Grammar point
Ordinal numbers (as used in dates)
first/second/third/fourth .../twenty-first etc.

Method

1   Check students know ordinal numbers (up to 31st) and remind them that these are used for dates in English. Revise pronunciation of letters G H I J K L .

2   As Activity 5 but students ask each other the question *What's the date in square ...?*

3   When a pair has finished, they put up their hands and remain silent. It is up to you when you stop the game. You might like to let the first three pairs finish, depending on the size of the class, or you may prefer to continue until most people have finished.

4   For feedback, draw the grid on the board and invite six students to come out and fill in the columns, as directed by their partners. While this is going on, students see how accurate they were (students can exchange papers for checking).

5   You could extend this activity by asking students to think of a date they consider important. Each person then says it and others write it down and then try to guess why it is important.

7   Four people

Time: 20 minutes
Type of activity: Information gap activity with students working in pairs
Preparation: Make one copy of the handouts on pages 47 and 48 per pair of students (A and B)

Grammar points
Asking *WH-* questions in the present simple tense
What is ...?/Where does ...?/What does ...?/ How many ...?
Answering questions using the present simple tense
X lives .../comes from .../likes .../dislikes ...

Method

1   Divide the class into pairs. You might like to put a stronger student with a weaker one and try to make students work with a variety of different partners over the year.

2   Give one person in each pair Student A's handout and the other person Student B's handout.

3   Explain that they have in front of them the CVs of four people, but these CVs are incomplete. They are going to complete them by asking each other questions.

Check they know what kind of questions to ask and write some on the board if necessary to help them. (Rub these off once the activity is under way.)

4 Set a time-limit (ten minutes) and see if they can finish by then. Circulate as they are working to give any help necessary with vocabulary.

5 Stop the activity and let students compare their sheets to see how well they have done.

6 Now give them two minutes to memorise the sheet. During this time, write the four names on the board. Then ask them to turn their sheets over and see what they remember. This can be done individually or in teams.

7 For an extension activity, you might like to ask them which of the four people they would most like to meet and if they were looking for a new teacher, which one they would choose and why.

8 Half a crossword: Irregular verbs

Time: 20 minutes
Type of activity: Information gap with students working in pairs or groups of four
Preparation: Make one copy of the handouts on pages 49 and 50 per group/pair

Grammar point
Irregular verbs: infinitive and past tense
e.g. *eat/ate; break/broke; say/said; tell/told*

Method

1 You might like to start with a brainstorming session where the class give you all the past tenses they know of both regular and irregular verbs.

2 Divide class into small groups (2–4) and give half the group handout A and the other half handout B. Allow a few minutes for students to look at the verbs and check that they know the infinitive form. Help if necessary. On no account should they look at the other crossword.

3 Check everyone knows how a crossword works and teach *across* and *down* with some examples: *What's 4 across? What's 18 down?* etc.

4 Explain that they are going to ask questions to complete their crossword and will also answer questions. They must answer by saying 'It's the past tense of *(infinitive)*' and not the actual word, so that the other group have to work it out.

5 The members of the group now face each other and take it in turns to ask the questions to find the verbs that are missing from their crosswords.

6 You can either stop the game after a certain time whether they have finished or not, or you may prefer to continue until most have finished.

7 Students then compare crosswords and check to see if they got any verbs wrong.

8 For a follow-up activity, you could ask students to see how many of the verbs they remember (there were 44 in the crossword).

9 A day the life of . . .

Time: 20–25 minutes
Type of activity: Pair work with information gathering and talking about oneself
Preparation: Make one copy of the handout on page 51 per pair of students and cut it into two

Grammar points
Asking questions about times and regular habits, using the present simple tense
What time do you ...?/When do you ...?
Talking about clock times
at seven thirty/at a quarter to twelve, etc.
Describing daily routine, using the present simple tense and adverbs of frequency
I usually get up at .../I normally have lunch at .../I always go to bed at ...

Method

1 Divide the class into pairs (A and B) and give each each student the appropriate handout.

2 Explain that they are going to find out about their partner's daily routine, but first they are going to imagine what a typical day in their partner's life would be like.

3 They work individually to fill in the clock faces and say what they imagine their

partner would typically do at that time. They should fill in the name of their partner at the top of the sheet then use what they know and their imagination. Leave time for this to be completed.

4   Revise the type of question they might want to ask and how to reply, using adverbs of frequency where appropriate. If you consider it necessary, also revise clock times.

5   Now give pairs about ten minutes to ask each other questions to see how accurate they were in their predictions.

6   Have a class feedback, asking each pair how accurate they were and which fact about their partner's daily life most surprised them.

10 Neighbours

Time: 15–20 minutes
Type of activity: Find the differences between two pictures in pairs
Preparation: Make copies of the handouts on pages 52 and 53 per pair of students

Grammar point
Present continuous tense
Asking questions
e.g. *What's the man/woman/girl, etc. doing in flat 5?*
Are the people in flat 10 having a party?
Answering questions
She's ironing./No, he's mending his bicycle.
Giving information
The man in flat 3 is having breakfast., etc.

Method

1   Divide the class into pairs – try to get people to work with somebody they have not worked with before if possible.

2   Explain that they each have a picture of a big block of twenty flats, but the pictures are from different times of day and there are a number of differences between them. By asking each other questions they are going to try to find all the differences.

3   Give out the handouts and tell students to keep theirs a secret from their partner.

Revise the present continuous (form and use) with a quick sketch on the board of somebody singing at their window and asking *What's she doing? Is she singing?*

4   Give them about ten minutes to find as many differences as they can. At this stage, do not say how many differences there are.

5   Ask how many differences they have found. If necessary, tell them there are eight and give further time for them to be found.

6   Students then compare their pictures and see if they were correct.

7   As a follow-up activity, give each pair one of the characters. They try and imagine as much as they can about this person and then present a brief description to the class. A variation on this would be to give the same person to several groups and then compare what they came up with.

11 Up, down, left, right

Time: 20–30 minutes
Type of activity: Giving and receiving instructions in pairs
Preparation: Make copies of pages 54 and 55 per pair of students

Grammar points
Using the imperative to give instructions
start, go, copy
Prepositions
in, up, down, left, right, above, below

Method

1   Revise prepositions *up, down, left, right* using arrows on the board. Then draw two stars to revise *above, below.*

2   Divide the class into pairs (A and B) and give each student the appropriate handout. They must keep this sheet a secret from each other.

3   If necessary, revise the names for the ten objects on the sheet.

4   Student A starts by reading the instructions 1–6 out loud to Student B, slowly enough for Student B to follow them and draw the object in the appropriate square. Student A can repeat the instructions but must not

point to the correct square or give any other help.

5   When this is finished, students change roles and it is now Student B's turn to read out their instructions (1–6) for Student A to follow.

6   When both have finished, they look at the answer on each other's sheets.

7   As a follow-up, ask students to draw in five more objects in their answer grid (these could be the same objects or completely new ones). Then they find a new partner and give this partner instructions. This is good practice of the grammar points as of course they have to use the imperatives and prepositions in their own sentences.

8   This could be extended to homework where they make up grids and write the instructions.

12 A country scene

Time: 20–25 minutes
Type of activity: Giving and following instructions, in pairs
Preparation: Make a copy of page 56 per pair of students and cut it into two

Grammar points
Prepositions of place
in front of, behind, next to, beside
Giving instructions using the imperative
draw, copy

Method

1   Tell the class that they are going to be artists and write the following words on the board: *bird, bridge, chimney, cloud, curtains, dog, door, man fishing, grass, mountain, river, road, smoke, tree, window.*

    Ask individual students to come up and illustrate the words (quick sketch) or you may prefer to read them out and ask students to draw them and then check understanding.

2   Divide the class into pairs – Student A talks and Student B draws. Let them choose the role they prefer.

3   Give handout A to Student A (the talker) and handout B to Student B (the artist).

Emphasise that Student A must keep the completed picture a secret from Student B. However, Student A can look at what Student B draws, but must only look and on no account touch the paper.

4   Now Student A tells his/her partner what to draw and where to draw it, using the imperative and prepositions of place, e.g. *Draw a man beside the bridge; Draw another tree next to the first tree*, etc. If necessary, write a few examples on the board, rubbing them off when the activity has got under way.

5   When they have finished, let them compare drawings. You might like to pass round the pictures or hold them up and get the class to choose the best artist.

Elementary/ Pre-intermediate

13 Do you know me well?

Time: 20–25 minutes
Type of activity: Pair work with whole class feedback
Preparation: Make a copy of page 57 per pair of students and cut it into two

Grammar points
Asking questions in the present tense, using a variety of auxiliaries
Do you ...?/Have you got ...?/Are you ...?/Can you ...?
Giving short answers, using the appropriate auxiliary, positive and negative
Yes, I am./Yes, I can./Yes, I have.
No, I don't./No, I haven't./No, I'm not.
Using present tenses to give information
X likes .../Y can .../Z hasn't got ...

Method

1   As an introduction, ask the class how well they think they know you. Write three or four of the questions from the handout on the board, choosing any that you feel might give your students problems, e.g. *Do I think fashion is a waste of money?/Am I good with money?* Invite them to note down *Yes* or *No* and then to ask you the questions.

    Explain that they are now going to see how well they know their class mates.

2   Divide the class into pairs – A and B. Try to

separate best friends so students work with somebody they do not know that well and will have to speculate about. Give each student the appropriate handout. Revise the question forms and short answers, drawing students' attention to the auxiliaries they should use.

3   At first they work alone to read each sentence and make a prediction, trying to guess what their partner's answer will be. They do this by putting a cross in the appropriate column. Leave a few minutes for this, circulating to give help where needed.

4   When both students are ready, they turn to face each other and take it in turns to ask the questions and check if they have guessed correctly. If they were right, they put a tick in the final column. If they were wrong, they should try to note down some details of the correct answer.

5   If some pairs finish early, encourage them to ask each other for more details while waiting for the rest of the class.

6   Have a whole class feedback, asking for who made the most accurate predictions. You could ask each student to give the class one interesting or surprising fact about their partner.

7   This activity could be extended to make a class profile. You could also ask students to make up their own questionnaires for homework and then use them in class.

14 Can you follow instructions?

Time: 15 minutes
Type of activity: Understanding and following instructions, with a race to finish first
Preparation: Make one copy of page 58 per student

Grammar points
Imperative forms as used in giving instructions
Draw .../Write .../Cross out .../Underline ...
Following instructions using prepositions of place
left-hand/above/in front of/around

Method

1   This is a fun activity which will give students plenty of practice in close and careful reading and they will be doing a comprehension exercise without realising it. There is also the added fun element of trying to finish first.

2   Explain to the class that they are going to take part in a game that will see who is best at following instructions. Give everyone a copy of the handout and give a few minutes for them to read it through and ask you to explain any words they do not understand. No one is to write anything during this time.

3   Tell everyone to get ready and explain that they will have exactly five minutes to fill in the sheet and must not start until you say 'Start' and stop immediately you say 'Stop'. Build up a bit of atmosphere and when everyone is ready, shout 'Start'.

4   Students now work alone to fill in the handout while you circulate to give any help needed with comprehension.

5   After exactly five minutes, shout 'Stop' and students must stop whether they have finished or not.

6   Take in all sheets and redistribute (they are named so can be given back later). Put students into small groups (4–6) and ask them to compare their answers in the group and mark the sheets. Allow some time for this.

7   Do a whole class feedback to check answers and ask students to write the score on the handout they are correcting and hand it back. Congratulate the class champions.

8   For a further activity, students work together in groups to write their own instructions, finishing these for homework. You could use some in class!

Key

The answer for question 11 is 9,348. The answer for question 17 is 30 – 'left-hand' counts as one word and '2' doesn't count as a word.

15 Make a sentence – score a point!

Time: 10 minutes for each verb sheet
Type of activity: Board game for group work
Preparation: Make copies of the two verb handouts on pages 59 and 60 per group of 4/5 students

Make one copy of the number
cards on page 61 per group and
cut them out

Grammar point
Past tense of irregular verbs
went/lost/sold/ate, etc.
Use the verbs to make short sentences about
the past
I bought a new pair of trainers last weekend.

Method

1   Divide the class into small groups of about
    four or five students and ask them to sit
    together. Give each group the first verb
    handout and the numbers (1–16). They put
    the handout in front of them on the table.
    They shuffle the numbers and then place
    these face down on the table.

2   The group take it in turns to pick a number
    and then look at the verb in that square.
    They must then make up a sentence using
    that verb in the past tense e.g. *Last summer
    I flew to Spain* (when the verb *fly* was in the
    square of the number picked).

    The reason for using the number cards is
    that it creates a certain amount of suspense
    as nobody knows which square is going to
    be next. This usually results in everyone
    paying great attention!

3   The rest of the group have to decide
    whether the sentence is correct or not. If
    they decide it is correct, the verb is crossed
    out and the student's name is written in
    the box. Play now continues with the next
    person.

4   Once all the squares have been filled in,
    the student whose name appears most
    often is declared the winner of the first
    round.

5   Now everyone is warmed up, proceed to
    the second round, giving out the second
    verb handout. Students use the number
    cards again. You can either keep the same
    groups or make new ones.

6   The game is broadly similar but this time
    students need to make up true sentences,
    either about themselves or somebody they
    know! Also if the other students do not
    think the sentence is correct, they must ask

you. If it turns out to be correct, the
student concerned gets an extra point.

7   You could also add an extra point for two
    squares in a row and deduct a point for a
    wrong sentence. In fact it would be an
    interesting exercise to ask students for their
    own ideas as to how else the game could
    be played and scored. Certainly everyone
    should know the past tense of these 32
    irregular verbs when you have finished!

16   I like this but I don't like that!

Time: 20 minutes
Type of activity: Whole class mingle, asking and
                    answering questions
Preparation: Make copies of pages 62 and 63
                    so each student gets one card

                    Cut up each handout into eight
                    separate cards

Grammar points
Expressing likes and dislikes followed by a noun
I like cats./I love parties./I hate opera.
Expressing likes and dislikes followed by a gerund
*I love going to the dentist/I hate flying/I like getting
up early.*
Asking questions about likes and dislikes
Do you like ...?/Do you hate ...?
Short answers
Yes, I do/No, I don't.

Method

1   Introduce the topic by writing LIKES and
    DISLIKES on the board and asking for
    suggestions as to what to list under each
    heading. Point out that nouns or gerunds
    can be used and encourage students to
    make whole sentences, using a range of
    verbs: *like/love/dislike/don't like/hate.*

2   Give each student one of the cards (numbers
    do not have to be equal but all the cards 1–8
    must be used). Point out that on the card,
    they have pictures showing one thing they
    like and one thing they don't like. They
    need to form the sentences correctly e.g. *I
    like going to the dentist. I hate listening to pop
    music.* Tell everyone to pick up a pen or
    pencil and stand up.

3   They now participate in a whole class
    mingle, walking round and questioning
    other students about their likes and

dislikes, asking *Do you like ...?* and *Do you dislike ...?* The object is to find out the names of students who like and dislike the two items written on their cards and note these down.

4   After about five minutes, stop the activity. Ask who has managed to fill in their card and ask each student to tell you one thing they found out.

5   The activity can be extended by asking students what they remember of the eight items that were liked and the eight that were disliked. List these on the board and see which one is genuinely the most liked by the class and which the most disliked.

17 A family tree

Time: 15–20 minutes
Type of activity: Problem-solving by sharing information in groups
Preparation: Make copies of page 64 per group of 6 students

Cut out the six cards at the bottom of the handout

Grammar points
Using the present simple to talk about family relationships
X is Y's mother-in-law./Z is an only child./W has two sons.
Using the present simple and indefinite article to talk about jobs
V is a doctor./U's mother is a nurse.
Use of apostrophe *'s* to show possession
D is C's grandfather/P's nephew.

Method

1   If you feel it would be useful, draw a quick family tree on the board (perhaps of a famous person or somebody the class will know about) to revise family relationships and the use of the apostrophe *s*.

2   Divide the class into groups of six. Give each group a copy of the family tree and give each person in the group one of the information cards. If groups are smaller, one or more students will need to have more than one information card. Each group must have all six cards. The group chooses one person to fill in the family tree.

3   Students now take it in turns to read out the information they have on their cards. They can only read this and must not show it to the others. This encourages good pronunciation and careful listening! They should read a sentence each and start to fill in the family tree. Encourage them to listen to quite a lot of the information before writing anything and to use a pencil rather than a pen as they may want to change what they have written as they start to work things out.

4   Once most groups have finished, stop the activity and do a feedback to check. You could copy the family tree onto the board and then ask a representative from each group to come up and fill in a part according to instructions from their group.

5   This could lend itself to further class work and homework. Students could draw and describe their own family tree or may prefer to make one up.

Key

Row 1:	Douglas, Sylvia
Row 2:	Sally, Mark, David, Anne, Peter, Nina
Row 3:	nurse, electrician, accountant, editor, teacher, doctor
Row 4:	Amanda, Bob (or Tom), Tom (or Bob), Joanna (or Rebecca), Rebecca (or Joanna)

18 Left, right, up, down

Time: 20 minutes
Type of activity: Giving and receiving instructions in pairs
Preparation: Make copies of pages 65, 66 and 67 per pair of students

Grammar points
Using prepositions
up, down, right, left, in, below, above
Using the imperative to give instructions
go left/go up/draw/start/write

Method

1   Divide the class into equal numbers of As and Bs (if there is an odd number, that student should be a B and work in a group of three with one A and two Bs). Give the As the two handouts entitled 'Student A'

and send them to a part of the classroom to work together to fill in the grid, following instructions 1–8 in the box at the top of the sheet. They should then read, silently, through the second set of instructions 1–13 and check they understand everything, asking each other quietly for clarification if necessary.

2   Meanwhile give Bs the empty grid and explain that they are going to fill this grid with words and pictures, following Student A's instructions. Check that they all know how to draw the following items by asking individuals to come up to the board to draw: comb/triangle/candle/lamp/pair of scissors/fish/clock/chair/apple/cross.

3   Now make pairs with one A and one B. They sit so that Student B cannot see Student A's grid or instructions. Student A reads out the instructions 1–13 and Student B follows them, asking for repetition if necessary. Student A is not allowed to say the number of the square but should be ready to repeat slowly what is written. Student B should use a pencil as s/he may need to make some alterations.

4   Circulate while all this is going on to give help where needed. When students have completely finished, allow them to look at each other's grids to see how well they match.

5   When most pairs have finished, bring the activity to a close and check the answers by calling out random numbers of squares and asking what should be in them. Congratulate those who have managed to fill in the grid correctly.

19 True or false?

Time: 20 minutes
Type of activity: Find someone activity, in groups
Preparation: Make a copy of page 68 per student

Grammar points
Asking questions in various tenses
Have you ...?/Did you ...?/Were you ...?/Are you ...?
Short answers, using auxiliaries
Yes, I have./No, I didn't./No, I'm not.
Using determiners
more/most/half/least

Method

1   Divide class into groups (6–9 students) and give each student a copy of the handout. Get groups to sit together.

2   Go through the questions with the whole class asking them to tick True if they think the fact is true or False if they think the fact is false for the people in their group. They only guess at this stage and must not talk to each other.

3   Now go through the questions, making sure that students know how to ask the appropriate question to find out if they are right or not e.g. *Have you visited Rome?/Did you watch the news on TV last night?* etc. Draw their attention to the different tenses.

    When you have worked through the questions, briefly practise short answers e.g. *Yes, I have./No, I didn't.* etc.

4   Now students question others in their group to see how accurate they were in their predictions. They should use the boxes on their handouts to write in brief details of anyone who answered *Yes*.

5   Students compare their answers with what they predicted and discuss the results as a group.

6   Have a whole class feedback asking students to report on one or two facts they found interesting or surprising. At this stage, encourage the use of the determiners by writing on the board: *most/some/at least ... people/only one/half* and asking students to try to make sentences about their results.

20 Find the differences

Time: 15–20 minutes
Type of activity: Find the differences, working in pairs
Preparation: Make one copy of pages 69 and
                 70 per pair

Grammar points
Present continuous tense
The woman is talking on a mobile phone./The girl is doing her homework./The dog is eating the dinner.
There is/There are
There is a television in the room./There are five people.
Asking questions
How many people are there?/Is the man reading a

newspaper?/What is the dog doing?
Prepositions of place
The girl is beside the woman./The dog is under the chair.

Method

1   Divide the class into pairs (A and B) and give each student the appropriate handout. They must keep their handout hidden from their partner at all times.

2   Let them look at their pictures and write on the board any vocabulary you think they might need. If you think it necessary, revise the use of the present continuous to describe what is happening at a specific time and suggest a few ways of asking questions e.g., *How many .../What .../Is .../Where ...?* etc.

3   Now pairs ask each other questions to see if they can find all the differences between their pictures. Tell them that they can only answer questions from their partner but should not give extra information. Set a five-minute time-limit.

4   Circulate to give help and encouragement. (It can also be useful to listen to the kind of language students are using and the mistakes they are making and then do a quick session on this at the end of the lesson.)

5   After five minutes, tell everyone to stop and ask how many differences they have found. Tell them there are fifteen so, unless the majority of the class has found all of them, give more time for pairs to try and find them all.

6   Finally allow students to look at each other's pictures to check. For a whole class feedback, ask them to turn the pictures over and then ask each pair to give you one difference they remember until all fifteen have been found.

21   What did you do last week?

Time: 20 minutes
Type of activity: Group role-play
Preparation: Make enough copies of pages 71 and 72 so that each student has one role-card (i.e. for up to 8, one copy of each handout, for up to 16,

2 copies of each, etc.)
Cut out individual role-cards

Grammar point
Past simple tense
went / thought / bought etc.
Asking questions about the past
Did you go to the cinema last Saturday?/What did you see?
Did you buy a car?/What sort of car did you buy?

Method

1   Divide the class into eight groups, numbered 1–8. Each member of the group is given the same role-card so all members of group 1 have a copy of role-card 1, etc.

2   Explain that each group has some information on their card about what they did on one day last week. They also have three things to find out about what other people in the class did.

3   Give them time to work as a group to decide what questions they need to ask to get the information they need. Correct and help as necessary.

4   When everyone is ready, arrange the students into new groups so that each group has at least one student from the original groups 1–8. If there are less than 16 students in your class, the whole class should work together as one group.

5   Now the role-play can begin. Students take it in turns to talk to different people in their new group, trying to find out the three missing pieces of information. When the groups are working, circulate to give help where needed. When you feel that most people have finished, stop the activity.

6   Ask each student to give you one piece of information they gathered and encourage the class to reconstruct what happened last week.

7   For an extension you could ask students to each tell you one real thing they did last week orally and then ask the whole class to write down as many as they can remember.

22   Do you have a good memory?

Time: 15 minutes
Type of activity: Teacher-led memory game

Preparation: Make one copy of page 73 per student

Grammar points
Using the present simple to answer questions
The door is open/It's twenty-five to twelve.
Using *There is/There are* in descriptions
There is a photograph./There are ten books.
Using prepositions of place
The photo is on the mantelpiece./The stereo is on the bottom shelf.

Method

1 Give each student a copy of the handout and give them three minutes to study it and memorize the scene. They are not allowed to speak or make any notes. While they are doing this, write any vocabulary items you feel might cause a problem on the board.

2 When the three minutes are up, students turn over their handouts and write the numbers 1–15 on a separate piece of paper.

3 Read out the following questions and give students time to write their answers:

  1 What time is it?

  2 How many cushions are there altogether?

  3 There is a painting on the wall. What does it show?

  4 Is there a television set in the bookcase? If so, on which shelf?

  5 There is a photograph on the mantelpiece. Who is in the photograph?

  6 How many armchairs are there?

  7 What is on the coffee table?

  8 Where is the door?

  9 Are there more than ten books on the bookcase?

  10 Describe any animals in the room.

  11 Is there a lamp in the room?

  12 What is on the bottom shelf of the bookcase?

  13 Where is the plant?

  14 How many magazines are there on the floor?

  15 Has the fire been lit?

4 Ask students to write their names on their papers and take them in. Then redistribute so that everyone has another person's work to mark.

5 Read out the questions again and ask students to give you the answers by looking at the picture. Award 1 point for each correct answer. Once the work is marked, (and the total points added up), it should be handed back and the memory champions congratulated.

6 As an extension activity, ask everyone to add five more details themselves to the picture and then give this to their partner to study for one minute. They then ask some questions to see what each other has remembered of this new picture.

7 Homework could be to write a certain number of sentences about the picture or describe their own living room at home (and illustrate).

23 Biographies

Time: 20–25 minutes
Type of activity: Information gap with students working in pairs
Preparation: Make a copy of pages 74 and 75 per pair of students

Grammar points
Past simple tense as used in biographies
He was born/He made/He saw/He died etc.
Asking *WH-* questions in the past tense
When did he ...?/Why did he ...?/What did he ...?
Time indicators
later/until/when/still/in
Spelling unknown words and names
How do you spell Braque? B-R-A-Q-U-E

Method

1 Write the word 'biographies' on the board and check students know what it means. Ask if they have read any and if so, whose. Then write the names 'Picasso' and 'David Livingstone' on the board and see what, if anything, they already know about these two men. Teach the words *artist* and *explorer* if necessary. Explain that they are now going to read mini-biographies of these two men.

2 Divide the class into pairs (A and B) and give each student the appropriate handout. Give them a few minutes to read through the passages. Point out that they all have twelve spaces to fill in, but that these are not the same spaces so they will have to work together to complete their biographies.

3 Draw their attention to the fact that biographies are written in the past (almost invariably!) so they will need to ask questions in the past to get the information they need from their partner. Practise some WH- questions e.g. *What did Picasso do in Spain? Why did David Livingstone go to Africa?* etc.

4 Explain that they will now have ten minutes to work together to fill in all the spaces in their biographies. They must do this by asking questions in turn and must aim to note down the information accurately if necessary, asking for words and especially proper names to be spelt. If necessary, practise *How do you spell that, please?* and the pronunciation of letters of the alphabet.

5 Now sit students facing their partners and give them exactly ten minutes to complete their passages. Stress that on no account are they to look at each other's handout and that information can only be given in answer to a question.

6 While they are working, circulate to give help where needed. If some students finish before the time is up, ask them to work together on a mini-biography of someone famous they know about.

7 Stop after ten minutes, whether everyone has finished or not. Students now work together in pairs to check their work. Do a whole class round-up by asking each student to give you one piece of information they remember (without looking at the handouts) and try to reconstruct both biographies.

8 If some students have prepared short biographies, ask them to read them to the class.

9 For extension work and homework, students could be asked to write mini-biographies of people of their choice, using these texts as models.

24 Life style surveys

Time: 30 minutes
Type of activity: Asking questions and collating information working as a class
Preparation: Make copies of pages 76 and 77 so that each student will have one mini-survey (i.e. for a class of 12 you need 2 copies of each page, etc.)

Grammar points
Asking set questions in the present simple
Do you go to the cinema?/Do you enjoy shopping?
Yes/No answers with frequency adverbs
Yes, always/No, never/No, hardly ever/Yes, sometimes.
Making statements using the present simple giving information using determiners
Most people try to keep fit./Hardly anyone enjoys cooking.

Method

1 Write the words 'life style survey' on the board and discuss what it means. Ask students if they have ever taken part in a survey and if so what it was for.

2 Explain that everyone is now going to take part in a class survey to find out about current life styles. Write the six topics on the board: sport/free time and entertainment/travel and holidays/food and drink/health/shopping (you might like to prolong this initial discussion by asking what questions they would expect to be asked and also what topics have not been covered).

3 Give each student one of the mini-surveys – try to make numbers as even as possible. Allow time for reading the questions and answering any questions about vocabulary. Draw their attention to the answer key and make sure everyone understands the six frequency expressions (*hardly ever* may cause problems).

4 Give them about ten minutes to go round the class interviewing six others and noting down their answers in the appropriate columns. Circulate yourself to give help where needed. Tell students not to answer questions on the same topic more than once.

5 When students have finished, they should sit down in a part of the classroom with

other students who have the same topic i.e. all those who have the topic 'health' sit together. Stop the activity after ten minutes or earlier if most students have completed their survey.

6   Students now work as a group to pool their results and write five sentences which reflect what they have found out on their topic. Write the following pattern on the board: *Everyone ...*
Most people ...
Almost everyone ...
Two/three people ...
Only one person ...
Hardly anyone ...
No one ...

7   Each group now reads out their results. Invite comments: are the results surprising in any way? When all groups have finished, ask them to suggest some conclusions: what does this suggest about today's life styles?

8   This could be followed up by a homework essay expressing both the results and some of the students' opinions.

Pre-intermediate/ Intermediate

25 Find someone who ...

Time: 25 minutes
Type of activity: Find someone who ... whole class mingle
Preparation: Make one copy of page 78 per student

Grammar points
Asking questions in the present perfect tense
Have you been to London?/Have you been frightened by a film?
Short answers using the present perfect
Yes, I have./No, I haven't.
WH- questions using the simple past
When did you go to London?/Which film frightened you?
Using the past simple to give information
I went to London in 1990./'The Mummy' frightened me.

Method
1   Give each student a copy of the handout. Go through the questions quickly to make sure everyone understands them. Point out the use of the present perfect and practise asking and answering questions with this tense: *Have you ...? Yes, I have/No, I haven't.*

2   Do one question completely as an example, showing how a follow-up question will use the simple past e.g.: *When did you go? What did you do? Where did you work?* etc.

3   Now give time for students to circulate round the room, finding answers to all the questions. They should question each person until they get a *yes* and then ask for further details. They note these details down on their sheets and then go on to ask another person. The object of the activity is to get a *yes* answer to each question.

4   Circulate while the activity is taking place to give help and encouragement when needed. Bring the activity to an end when you feel most people have finished or after fifteen minutes.

5   Do a whole class feedback, asking different students to give the answers. Ask for more details where appropriate.

6   When this has been done, you could ask the class to note down the answers that amused or surprised them. Can they make any generalisations about the profile of the class? You could also ask everyone to make up a further question to ask.

26 Conjunctions bingo

Time: 15 minutes per game
Type of activity: Teacher-led with students working individually
Preparation: Make one copy of pages 79 and 80 per ten students for each game

Cut Bingo cards up

Cut one set of Teacher's words up and put in a container (e.g. hat/cup/box, etc.)

Grammar points
Conjunctions of time
when/as soon as/as long as/while, etc.
Other conjunctions
although/even if/whether, etc.

Method

1 Revise conjunctions and how to use them if you think this is useful for your class. You could write two sentences on the board and ask students to join them together e.g.

She was tired. + She went to bed. = She was tired so she went to bed/She went to bed when she was tired/She went to bed because she was tired/As she was tired she went to bed.

She was tired. + She didn't go to bed. = Although she was tired, she didn't go to bed/She didn't go to bed even though she was tired/In spite of being tired, she didn't go to bed.

Ask students to identify the conjunctions and say what their functions are.

2 Give each person a bingo card and allow a few minutes for everyone to read through their sentences and try to work out what conjunction could be missing from each one.

3 Now draw a word out of your container and say it out loud. As each conjunction is read out, students write it in one of the spaces on their card if appropriate.

4 Continue until one student has completed all five sentences and shouted 'Bingo'.

5 Check by asking the winning student/students to read out their sentences with the conjunctions in place. Check that they have used the conjunction correctly and that it is one that has been called out.

6 You can play another game after this one to reinforce what has been learnt. Students could work in pairs and you could also ask the winning students to read out the conjunctions.

27 Where are the carrots?

Time: 15–20 minutes
Type of activity: Problem solving by sharing information in groups

Preparation: Make one copy of page 81 per four students

Cut out the four information cards on each copy

Grammar points
Prepositions of place
above/between/on the right/next to, etc.
Describing where things are, using the present simple tense
The apples are in the same column as the peaches./The plums are in the bottom right-hand corner.

Method

1 Start by revising names of fruit and vegetables. Ask half of the class to list all the fruit they know and the other half to list the vegetables. Then ask them to read these out while you list them on the board. Check that students know the meanings – you could ask students to come up and draw them. Make sure that all those used in the activity have been mentioned but if not, draw them yourself and ask for the names.

2 Divide the class into groups of four. If any group has fewer students, one person will have to have two information cards; each group must have all four cards to be able to work out the puzzle. Give each group the top half of the handout with the picture of the stall and make sure they understand what it is. Make sure students understand the difference between a column and a row.

3 Now give out the information cards and explain that each person must keep their card a secret from everyone else. They must take it in turns to read out a sentence and work together to fill in the names of the fruit and vegetables. Each group should choose a secretary to do the writing. Encourage the secretaries to use pencil so that they can erase any mistakes easily.

4 While they are working, circulate to encourage clear reading and careful listening.

5 When most groups have finished, stop the activity and ask the question: *Where are the carrots?* (See below for answers) Draw a

15

blank stall on the board and write in the fruit and vegetables as students direct you.

Key

Row

1	plums	lettuce	apples	sprouts
2	cabbage	oranges	CARROTS	pineapples
3	peaches	cucumbers	grapes	potatoes

28 Four people's diaries

Time: 20 minutes
Type of activity: Find the differences working in pairs
Preparation: Make copies of pages 82 and 83 for half the class

Grammar point

Using the present continuous with future meaning for a planned activity
Next Thursday Peter is visiting his aunt.
Asking questions using the present continuous
Is Colin visiting his grandparents on Wednesday?/What is Emma doing on Thursday?
Answering questions
Yes, he is./No, he isn't./He's meeting his Dad for lunch.

Method

1   Ask the class if they have any plans for the weekend and what they are doing. Encourage them to use the present continuous tense for planned activities in the future. You might like to write up some fictional diary entries for yourself for the coming week as an example.

2   Divide the class into pairs (A and B) and give each student the appropriate handout. Explain that they both have the same people's diaries for the same week but that there are differences between them. They have to ask each other questions to find out the differences and circle them. Discuss the kind of question they should ask and write one or two examples up on the board e.g. *Where is Colin going on Tuesday?/Is Emma having lunch with Nick on Thursday?/What time is Helen taking the cat to the vet on Thursday?*

3   Now give ten minutes maximum for the pairs to work together to find all the differences. Circulate to give help where

needed. When a pair say they have finished, ask them how many differences they have found. There are eleven altogether, so you can encourage them to keep looking if they have fewer.

4   Stop the activity and ask for feedback, doing a diary at a time.

5   For follow-up work, give out the name of a famous person and ask the class to imagine their diary for the following week. This could be done in pairs and then exchanged with another pair.

6   For homework, students could choose a person of their choice and write a week in their diary.

29 Trace the route

Time: 15 minutes
Type of activity: Giving and receiving instructions in pairs
Preparation: Make copies of pages 84 and 85 per pair of students

Grammar points

Giving directions using the imperative
Go straight ahead./Turn left, etc.
Asking questions
Do I turn left or right?/Where do I go now?
Using adverbs and prepositions
You are in front of the post office./Go straight on.

Method

1   Revise directions if you think it necessary, for example, ask the class to direct you from where you stand to the staff room/entrance hall/head teacher's office, etc.

2   Divide the class into pairs and give Student A and Student B the appropriate handout. Student A must keep his/her handout a secret from Student B. Explain that Student A is going to direct Student B to a secret place in the town and Student B must trace the route on the map. Encourage the use of pencil so that mistakes can be rectified easily.

3   Now direct everyone to the station and allow five minutes. Circulate during this time to give help and encouragement and to make sure that those with the route are

not showing or pointing but only using words.

4   Stop the activity and ask Student B where they are.

5   To extend the activity, ask Student B in each pair to trace another route starting at the hospital. Then allow five minutes for them to describe this to Student A. This gives both people a chance to speak.

6   As a follow-up activity, you could choose a place in your town and ask students to write directions from there to some other place. They could then read these out and see if the rest of the class can follow them.

30 Group opinions

Time: 25 minutes
Type of activity: Find someone who ... group work
Preparation: Make one copy of page 86 per student

Grammar points
Tag questions
You don't trust politicians, do you?
You get depressed in the winter, don't you?
Short answers
Yes, I do./No, I'm not., etc.
Using expressions of number and amount
Most of us .../None of us .../A few of us ...

Method

1   Divide the class into groups (5–8). Give each student a copy of the handout.

    Explain that they have to interview every member of their group to find out their opinions on various subjects, e.g. how many of the group trust politicians, etc. However, instead of asking direct questions, they have to ask a tag question each time.

2   Do some examples of tag questions on the board e.g. *You prefer tea to coffee, don't you ? You don't like mobile phones, do you?* Check that everyone can make tag questions correctly before you start the activity.

3   Students now interview the other members of their group and make a note of the number of people who agree with the statement by putting ticks (✔) in the boxes

numbered 1–8. (There is no need for them to note the person's name.)

4   When they have finished, they add up the ticks next to each statement and from this work out how many of the group do the various things. They should now write twelve statements about what they have found out, using the words at the bottom of the page e.g., *None of us trusts politicians./Some of us get depressed in winter.,* etc.

5   Do a full class feedback by asking groups for their answers and comparing them. Did all groups more or less feel the same? If there were any big differences, what could have caused them?

6   To extend the activity, ask each group to come up with two or three other questions which they could ask another group or the class as a whole.

31 Arrange the furniture

Type of activity: Giving and following instructions in groups
Preparation: Make one copy of the main layout, page 89.

                   Make one copy of pages 87 and 88 per group of four students.

                   Cut out the objects at the top of page 88 and if possible stick them on to card (or photocopy them onto thin card)

Grammar points
Imperatives
Put/Move/Change etc.
Prepositions and adverbs
next to/beside/left, etc.
Comparatives
nearer/not so close/further away, etc.

Method

1   Divide the class into groups of four. Give each group one copy of the empty room on page 87, the various items of furniture cut out and the key to the furniture on page 88. Make sure everyone knows the words and can pronounce them correctly.

2   Explain that you have the master layout of the room and that the object of the game

is for each group to try to copy this layout as closely as they can.

3   Place the master layout on your desk with its back to the class (you can stick it onto card if you like).

4   One person from each group now comes up to your desk and studies the master layout for thirty seconds.

5   Then they go back to their group and without touching anything themselves tell the rest of the group where to place the furniture. (They obviously won't remember everything.)

6   Let a few minutes pass, then get the next person in the group to come out. Again they look at the master layout for thirty seconds and then go back to their respective groups.

7   This activity continues until all four students have been out to the front. Finally each group can choose one student who comes out for a final look.

8   Now go to each group in turn to see how well they have done. Award them a mark out of ten for their efforts.

9   You can extend this activity by getting each group to arrange the furniture in a different way and then describe this to another group.

32   What do they have in common?

Time: 20–25 minutes
Type of activity: Teacher-led activity – making comparisons in groups
Preparation: Make one copy of page 90 per group of 3–4 students

Grammar points
Comparisons between two items using *both ... and ...*
You blow both a flute and a trumpet.
Using *neither ... nor ...*
Neither drums nor trumpets have strings.

Method

1   Write the following six words on the board: *bull cat lion mouse snake spider* and ask *What do they have in common?* Tell students they have to think of as many

things as possible that pairs of words have in common. Give an example using *Both ... and ...* e.g. *Both a bull and a lion have a tail* and another example using *Neither ... nor* e.g. *Neither a snake nor a spider has four legs.* See how many other examples they can come up with.

2   Divide class into groups (3–4 students) and give each group a copy of the handout. Start by identifying the different items.

3   Now give them about ten minutes to write five sentences about each set of words, finding what pairs have in common, using *both* and *neither*.

4   When everyone has finished, go through a set at a time. Ask one group to read out their sentences. If no other group has got the same idea, they get a point for this. Continue with the other groups, marking the score on the board. Then go on to the next set. The group with the highest score wins!

33   Prepositions bingo

Time: 15 minutes per game
Type of activity: Teacher-led with students working individually
Preparation: Make enough copies of pages 91 and 92 for every member of class to have a Bingo card (make twice the number if you want to play two games)

Cut the Bingo cards out

Cut up one set of the Teacher's words on page 92 and put them into a container (so that you can draw them out one by one)

Grammar points
Prepositions of place
on the third floor/to the station
Prepositions of time
at eight o'clock/on Friday
Prepositions following verbs
proud of/work for

Method

1   Ask the class to tell you all the prepositions they know and use them in sentences. It is not easy to use prepositions correctly in

English and it is usually necessary to look at lots of examples and learn them. This is where Bingo is such a useful activity. Although teachers may get tired of it, students rarely do and for sheer concentration, there are few activities that can beat it!

2   Give everyone a Bingo card and give them a few minutes to read through the five sentences and try to work out which preposition is missing each time.

3   Put the twenty squares into a container, draw them out one at a time and say the preposition aloud. Leave time for students to decide if it fits one of their sentences and to write it in the space.

4   When students have completed all five sentences, they shout 'Bingo'. Stop the game and ask them to read out the sentences. Check that the sentences are correct.

5   If wanted, play another game, giving students another card. This way they will have had plenty of practice in using the correct prepositions.

6   Finally, you could ask the class to tell you the twenty prepositions used in the game and write these on the board. Divide class into two. A student from one side picks a preposition and a student from the other side uses it in a sentence. Do this until all have been used, giving points for correct usage.

34 Two funny stories

Time: 15 minutes
Type of activity: Jigsaw reading activity in groups
Preparation: Make one copy of pages 93 and 94 per group of 3–5 students

Cut up the different parts individually and shuffle so that you have 29 different parts per group; it is useful to keep the parts together in an envelope

Grammar points
Sentence structure and word order
subject + verb + object etc.
Logical links

yet ... as ... so ... but ...
Reading comprehension
Oral story telling

Method

1   Divide class into groups (3–5 students) and sit them together round a desk or table. Give each group a whole set of cut up cards (i.e., the 29 individual cards from the two funny stories shuffled).

2   Explain that they have to sort out the cards to make two funny stories. They should assemble the stories in the correct order on the table in front of them and tell you when they have finished.

3   While they are working, circulate to give encouragement and help with any vocabulary problems.

4   When a group tell you they have finished, go over and read what they have done. If it is incorrect, give them some clues (e.g., you could tell them that there are 14 parts in Story 1 and 15 in Story 2). If it is correct, congratulate them and tell them you are going to ask them to act out one of the stories in front of the class in a moment. Let them choose which one they prefer. Ask the next group that finishes to prepare the other story. Help any groups who may be having difficulties.

5   Stop the activity when everyone is ready and ask the two groups to act out the stories. Other groups can be asked to tell the stories from memory after this.

6   For homework students could be asked to tell a funny story of their choice.

35 Life stories

Time: 15–20 minutes
Type of activity: Find the differences in pairs
Preparation: Make copies of pages 95 and 96 per pair of students

Grammar point
Asking a variety of questions using the past simple
Was Andrew Scott born on June 9th 1955?
When did he start work at a post office?
Short answers
Yes, he was./No, he didn't.

Giving information using the past simple
Julie Parker was an actress./His mother was an estate agent.

Method

1   Put students into pairs (A and B) and give each student the appropriate handout, which they must keep secret from each other. Give them a chance to read through their account of the life story of Andrew Scott.

2   Explain that there are twelve differences between the two accounts and the object of the activity is to be the first to find all twelve. To do this, they can ask their partner twenty questions, marking off a number each time their partner asks a question. If necessary, discuss the kind of question they can ask e.g. *When was Andrew Scott born? Was Andrew Scott born in Brighton?* etc.

3   They now start asking questions in turn and putting a circle round any differences they find and noting what they are. Remind them that they should only answer their partners' questions and not offer any extra information or say what they have found out themselves.

4   When students have found all twelve differences, they stop asking questions (but may still have to answer their partner's). If students get to twenty questions, they must stop anyway even if they haven't yet found all twelve differences.

5   When people have finished, do a whole class feedback to confirm the twelve differences and congratulate those who found them in the smallest number of questions. They were obviously very good at knowing what questions to ask and could have promising careers as interviewers!

36 What do you remember?

Time: 25–30 minutes
Type of activity: Oral work with board game; groups
Preparation: Make one copy of page 97 per group of 3–5 students

Grammar points

remember + gerund
I remember earning money by doing washing up.
I remember not liking the Maths teacher very much.
Questions with *remember*
What do you remember about ...?
What do you remember doing?
Past tense for talking about past events
I went abroad for the first time in ...
I didn't enjoy ...
used to + infinitive
I used to visit my grandparents every summer.

Method

1   Write on the board *What do you remember about being five years old?* and elicit answers. Note the construction *I remember* + gerund e.g., *I remember eating lots of jam sandwiches* and the construction *I used to* + infinitive e.g., *I used to wake up very early in the morning.* Revise these and encourage students to use them as well as the simple past when talking about their memories.

2   Divide class into small groups (3–5 students) and give each group one copy of the handout. Let them look at the different items and make sure everyone understands them.

3   The object of the game is to win as many squares as you can by speaking about the subject on it for one minute. Each person has a turn and is given a number by the rest of the group (they can choose this or it could be picked by chance). They then speak for a minute on this subject, being timed by a member of the group. If they manage to speak for one minute, they win that square and put their initials in it. If they stop speaking early, someone else can take over and if they are speaking when the minute is up, they win the square and put their initials in it. Play then passes to the next person until all the board is completed. The person with the most squares wins.

4   Note: if a minute seems rather long for your class, try thirty seconds. Also if you want to introduce an element of chance into the selection of the squares, put twenty pieces of paper numbered 1–20 in an envelope and let students choose one.

(Numbered pieces of paper like this can be useful for a variety of games.)

Intermediate/ Upper Intermediate

37 Are you the person I'm looking for?

Time: 20 minutes

Type of activity: Find somebody who ... whole class mingle

Preparation: Make enough copies of pages 98 and 99 for each student to have one card (i.e. one copy of each for a class up to twenty; two copies of each for up to forty)

Cut these up into individual cards (keeping sets of 20 together)

Grammar points
Asking questions
Using different auxiliaries and modals
Can you ...?/Would you ...?/Were you ...?/Have you ...? etc.
Short answers
Yes, I have./No, I don't./Yes I can., etc.
WH-questions
What ...?/When ...?
Using a variety of tenses

Method

1 This is an excellent activity to get all the students talking and using a wide variety of verb tenses and question structures. Give each student one card. Try to use as wide a variety as possible (there are 20 different ones). Allow a short time for them to work out what questions to ask.

2 Students now walk round the room, trying to find answers to the five questions on their cards. To ensure that they talk to as many people as possible, tell them that they are only allowed to ask one question every time they talk to someone.

3 Students write down any answers to their questions plus the name of the student who gave them the answer.

4 When most students seem to have got all their answers, stop the activity.

5 For a quick feedback, ask each student to tell you about one of the answers on their card. It might also be interesting to concentrate on any questions for which the students couldn't get answers and ask why.

38 Broken sentences

Time: 15–20 minutes

Type of activity: Jigsaw reading in small groups

Preparation: Make enough copies of pages 100 and 101 per group of 2–4 students

Cut up all broken sentences (you will have 40 items per set; be sure to keep whole sets together; use an envelope for storage)

Grammar point
Conjunctions
although/as/because/in case/so that/whatever/ unless, etc.
Positions of conjunctions
Although it was cold, we went out./We went out even though it was cold.
Use of conjunctions with verb or noun phrase
As long as you get paid, don't ask questions./In spite of being well-paid, he didn't enjoy his job.

Method

1 Divide the class into groups (2–4 students) and give each group a set of forty broken sentences. Give them time to work together to assemble the twenty complete sentences.

2 Circulate to help where necessary and check the answers of any group that has finished. Ask them to note down all the conjunctions while waiting for the others to finish.

3 When everyone has finished, go through the sentences, writing the conjunctions on the board.

4 Ask each group in turn to choose a conjunction from the list and use it in a new sentence. You can give points if you wish.

5 You could also ask students to try to remember the twenty original sentences from the activity (this gives them some very useful examples of usage).

6   Follow-on homework could be to write twenty sentences using the conjunctions on a subject of the student's choice.

39 Ask the right question

Time: 25–30 minutes
Type of activity: Oral activity, asking appropriate questions in groups
Preparations: Make enough copies of page 102 for every group of 4 students to have a set (there are 40 items in a set)

Cut up and keep sets together; store in an envelope

Grammar points
Asking *WH-* questions
What .../When .../Who ..., etc.
Using a variety of tenses and structures

Method

1   Divide the class into groups of four students. Within each group, pairs will play against each other (like in bridge for example). Extra students should make threes, to play against other threes or against pairs.

2   Give each group a set of 40 cards which are placed in a pile face down on the table.

3   One person starts by picking up a card which is not shown to anyone else. S/he must now ask a question that will make his/her partner say the word on the card. If the partner says the correct word, the card is shown to the group and placed in front of the person who said it. If the partner did not say the correct word, the card is put on the bottom of the pile, without being shown. In either case, play now passes to the other pair.

4   The activity continues until all the words have been said and all the cards given out. The pair with the most cards wins. Congratulate the class champions.

5   To continue the game ask students to write new words on the backs of the cards and then give these to another group to do.

40 The longest day

Time: 20–25 minutes
Type of activity: Teacher-led, intensive listening practice
Preparation: Make one copy of page 103 per student

Grammar point
A wide variety of past tenses
set out/drove/were sent/had left, etc.

Method

1   Give each student a copy of the handout. Explain that you are going to read a story with 28 missing verbs. The verbs are written on the handout and it is for the student to work out where they go.

2   Read out the following story, giving the number of each gap, but not the verb, and leaving students time to write in their verbs.

3   When you have finished, ask them to compare what they have written with a partner to see where they might have made mistakes. Then read the passage again.

4   For follow-up work, ask students to tell you the story or act it out in small groups. They could write it up for homework.

THE LONGEST DAY

This story happened a few years ago when British people could go on a day trip to France without a passport. It is about a Mr and Mrs Elham who went on a day trip to Boulogne.

When they (1 *... had finished ...*) their shopping, the couple (2 *... set out ...*) for a stroll to see the sights of the town. Unfortunately, they didn't (3 *... know ...*) much French and couldn't really (4 *... understand ...*) the street signs, so they (5 *... became ...*) completely lost. The French people they (6 *... met ...*) were very kind and eventually they (7 *... got ...*) a lift to the railway station.

As the last ferry (8 *... had left ...*), the Elhams (9 *... decided ...*) to go to Paris and (10 *... make ...*) their way back to Dover from there. Unfortunately, they (11 *... caught ...*) the wrong train and (12 *... found ...*) themselves the next morning – in Luxembourg! The local police (13 *... put ...*)

the confused passengers on a train for Paris and they (*14 ... slept ...*) most of the way – all too soundly in fact, for they (*15 ... missed ...*) their connection and (*16 ... woke up ...*) in Basel in Switzerland!

The obliging Swiss police (*17 ... gave ...*) the couple directions back to Boulogne but somehow they (*18 ... lost ...*) their way again and ended up (*19 ... hitchhiking ...*) over sixty kilometres to Vesoul in central France. A long-distance lorry driver gave the confused couple a lift to Paris, but when they (*20 ... reached ...*) the Gare du Nord, their troubles were not over.

'We (*21 ... misread ...*) the signs,' Mrs Elham (*22 ... explained ...*), 'and took the train to Bonn in Germany.'

From Germany the Elhams (*23 ... were sent ...*) quickly back to France. At the border, a sympathetic gendarme decided to (*24 ... make sure ...*) they got to Boulogne safely, so he (*25 ... drove ...*) them all the way there.

As they didn't have passports, it took twenty-four hours to (*26 ... persuade ...*) the Customs that their unlikely tale (*27 ... could ...*) possibly be true. But at last they were allowed on a ferry and soon the familiar white cliffs of Dover (*28 ... welcomed ...*) the Elhams back to England.

41 Old school friends

Time: 20–25 minutes
Type of activity: Role-play in pairs
Preparation: Make one copy of page 104 per pair of students and cut into two

Grammar points
was/were going to
You were going to be a pilot./I was going to be a doctor.
Asking questions about the past
Why didn't you become a pilot? Who did you marry?
Answering questions about the past
I never learnt to fly an aeroplane./I married Emma.

Method

1 Introduce the topic by saying something that you were going to do but didn't, e.g. *I was going to be an actress but my parents didn't approve, so I became a teacher. Now I'm glad as it's hard to get work acting and I don't think I'd have enjoyed it.* Write the *was going to* construction on the board as an

example. Ask the class if any of them have made plans that came true or didn't come true.

2 Divide the class into pairs (A and B) and explain that they are old school friends who meet each other by chance some years later at an airport. They ask each other lots of questions to see if the plans they made came true and if not, why not.

3 Give each student the appropriate handout and give them time to read it through and ask you for any explanations they need.

4 Now give them about ten minutes to talk to each other, using '*You were going to ... and did you ...?* Stress that they should use their imaginations to explain why they did or didn't actually do the various things they had planned.

5 After ten minutes, stop the activity whether students have finished or not. Ask each person to write five sentences about which of their partner's dreams did or didn't come true and why.

6 Do a whole class round-up by asking all the Student As: *Your old school friend was going to ... What happened and why?* Compare answers, writing up any particularly interesting ones. Then pass to the Student Bs.

7 This could lead on to a homework 'My old school friend'.

42 My ideal living room

Time: 15–20 minutes
Type of activity: Problem-solving as a group
Preparation: Make enough copies for each group of six students to have one copy of:
(i) the Students' copy (page 105)
(ii) the furniture (cut out) and key (page 106)
(iii) the layout (page 107)
(iv) the group cards (page 108)

Cut up the six cards

Cut out the furniture items

Store the complete set together, e.g. in a large envelope

Grammar points
Using prepositions of place in statements
The chair is in front of the desk./The sofa is not against the wall.
Giving and following instructions using the imperative
Put the sofa by the door./Place the plant next to the window.
Careful reading and listening

Method

1 Divide the class into groups of six. Odd students could make groups of seven or in groups without six members, one student will have to read out two cards.

2 Give each group the following: one copy of the Student's room; one set of furniture, cut out; the key to the furniture; a set of group cards cut up (do not give out the layout as this is the answer).

3 Groups put the empty room, furniture and key on the table in front of them. Each person takes one of the cards and keeps this a closely guarded secret – nobody else must see it.

4 They now take it in turns to read out the sentences on their cards and work as a group to arrange the furniture according to the information. When they have finished, they ask you to look. Compare what they have done with the completed room and give a mark out of ten. If it's less than ten, ask the group to choose a spokesperson. Give this spokesperson the handout of the completed room – s/he must not show the others nor offer information, but will answer their questions and help to correct any inaccuracies.

5 Bring the activity to a close and congratulate the class champions.

43 Trivia search

Time: 25–30 minutes
Type of activity: Information gap with a whole class mingle
Preparation: Make one copy of page 109 per six students

Grammar points
Asking a wide variety of questions, using different tenses

How long does a new-born baby spend crying?
Who designed the flag of Italy?
Explaining you don't know
I'm afraid I can't tell you./I've no idea.

Method

1 Give everyone in the class a card (numbers do not need to be equal but all cards must be used). Explain that they have three pieces of trivia and three questions to which they need to find answers. They should start by trying to imagine answers and noting these down on their cards.

2 Now spend some time suggesting ways in which they can reply when asked a question to which they do not have the answer. Note all their suggestions on the board and add some of your own if necessary e.g., *I don't know, I'm afraid./I really couldn't say./I have absolutely no idea./I'm sorry but I can't tell you.*, etc.

3 Students now circulate and ask and answer questions, either giving the information or saying they do not know. Let the activity continue until most people have finished. Then ask each person to tell you one thing they found out, covering all eighteen questions. See if anyone guessed or knew the answer before they were told.

4 Now ask everyone to find a partner and work together to try to remember as much of the trivia as they can (18 items). Congratulate the class memory champions!

44 Find the other half

Time: 20 minutes
Type of activity: Jigsaw reading in groups
Preparation: Make one copy of pages 110 and 111 per group of 3–4 students

                 Cut these up into half sentences (48 half sentences in all)

Grammar point
Prepositions used after adjectives
worried about/shocked at/jealous of/famous for

Method

1 Divide the class into groups (3–4 students). Each group should sit together round a

table large enough to assemble the sentences on.

2   Give each group the 48 half sentences and allow them time to assemble them into 24 whole sentences. Explain that they have to make sure that the correct preposition follows each adjective and that the sentence makes sense!

3   When everyone, or almost everyone, has finished, stop the activity. Ask each group in turn to read out a complete sentence. If it's correct, they get a point and that sentence cannot be said again. Continue until all sentences have been read out.

4   This is not an easy grammar point and some recycling is necessary. Divide class into teams. Read out the first half of a sentence and ask someone from team 1 to complete it. If it's correct, Team 1 gets a point. If not, Team 2 can try for a bonus point before having their turn.

5   For homework, you could give the beginnings of twenty sentences for students to finish in the most interesting way they can.

45 What sort of person are you?

Time: 25–30 minutes
Type of activity: Survey – asking for personal information in groups
Preparation: Make enough copies of pages 112–114 for every student to have one card (numbered 1–6)

Grammar points
Adverbs of frequency and the present simple
Making personal statements
I am usually calm./I frequently suffer from insomnia.
Reported speech
Everyone I spoke to said they were honest./Nobody said they were good with their hands.

Method

1   Put students into groups of six. Extra students can either make a smaller group or make some groups of eight.

2   Give each student in the group a different card 1–6. Give them a few minutes to read through the questions and put a tick in the first column if they answer *Yes*.

3   They now interview the others in their group putting ticks every time the answer is *Yes*.

4   When this oral part is over, students write sentences making generalisations based on their findings. Before they start, write an example or two on the board as a model e.g., *Everyone I spoke to said they were musical./Nobody I asked enjoyed being the centre of attention.* Draw students' attention to the rules of reported speech and the necessary tense changes.

5   Allow five minutes for this. Then ask all those who had Card 1 to read you their sentences. Did they all find the same? It could be interesting to speculate about any big differences. Continue with the other five cards and try to establish some kind of class profile.

6   If your class is interested, you might like to discuss the value of such questions and whether they are too personal. Also are we the best people to judge ourselves?

46 Strange but true

Time: 25–30 minutes
Type of activity: Information gap activity with students working in pairs
Preparation: Make one copy of pages 115 and 116 per pair of students

Grammar points
Language of supposition – modals
Queen Elizabeth I might have .../Indian ink could actually come from .../The corkscrew may have been invented to ...
Asking questions with a variety of forms and tenses
Why did ...?/What does ...?/What can't ...?

Method

1   Divide the class into pairs (A and B) and give each student the appropriate handout.

2   Explain that they are going to learn twenty amazing facts – ten are complete on their handout and ten are incomplete. Give them a few minutes to read through the facts and try to imagine what could be written in the spaces.

3   Now put each student with another student with the <u>same</u> handout. They compare what they have filled in and discuss possibilities. You might like to revise the language of speculation and the use of the modals *may/might/could* in the present and past tenses, e.g. *It may be true./They may have left./She might have done it./It could have been invented.*, etc. Write some examples on the board as models while they are speaking.

4   The next stage is to put this pair to work with another pair who have the <u>other</u> handout. They ask questions to find out the answers and compare these with what they originally thought. Once this is complete, tell them that five of the facts are completely untrue and the group of four now work together to decide which facts these are.

5   Have a whole class round-up and ask groups to say which facts they think are untrue and why.

6   For homework, ask students to choose five of the facts that particularly interested them and write a few lines about each.

Key

The following are untrue: numbers 3, 7, 10, 16 and 19.

47 Have you ever ...?

Time: 25–30 minutes
Type of activity: Questionnaire with students working in groups
Preparation: Make one copy of page 117 per student

Grammar points
Present perfect tense
Asking questions
Have you ever ...?
Using determiners to express number
Some of us .../None of us .../Most of us ...

Method

1   Ask students to form groups of four to six. Explain that they are going to see how much they know about one another.

2   Give each person a copy of the handout and go through explaining any problems.

3   Firstly students work alone to make a supposition about how many people in their group will answer *Yes* to each question. They write this number in the *How many?* column. When this has been done, ask each student to make one prediction – the one they feel most confident about perhaps – and write these up on the board.

4   Now give time for students to work in their groups, asking questions and filling in the final column – either by writing *Yes* if their prediction was correct or if not, writing the correct number. Circulate during this time to give help if needed.

5   Once this is over, students fill in the beginning of each sentence, choosing the appropriate words from the list at the top of their handout e.g. *All of us have failed a test./None of us has won money in a competition.*, etc.

6   Finally, look at the initial predictions again and congratulate those who guessed correctly – they obviously know their fellow students well!

48 Getting to know you

Time: 25–30 minutes
Type of activity: Question and answer activity with students working in pairs
Preparation: Make one copy of pages 118 and 119 per pair of students

Grammar points
Asking questions
What does this date mean?/Who is this?/Is this a place you like?
Giving information
This is the year I was born./This is a job I would really like to do.
Fluency practice

Method

1   Divide the class into pairs (A and B) and give each student the appropriate handout. Give them about five minutes to fill in the diagram with the answers to the questions. Circulate round the class while they are doing this to give help where needed.

2   When students have completed their diagram, they work with someone who has

the other handout. They should fold the sheet in half and show each other their diagrams only. They should take it in turns to ask and answer questions and speculate and give details about the answers. The aim is to make your partner talk as much as possible.

3   If the class is talking well, let this part continue for fifteen minutes. Otherwise stop after ten minutes. Have a whole class round-up asking each person to share with the class one interesting fact they found out about their partner.

4   If you want to continue the activity, ask each person to think of an answer e.g. *Snowy* and then ask the class, either individually or in teams, to guess what it refers to e.g. *Is Snowy the name of your dog?*

Upper Intermediate/ Advanced

49 House share

Time: 30–40 minutes
Type of activity: Simulation in groups
Preparation: Make one copy of page 120 per pair of students and cut into two

Grammar points
Asking and answering questions
How is the cleaning organised?
We're near the main shopping centre.
Fluency practice – appropriacy and communicative skills

Method

1   Start by talking about where students live and where they think they might live in the future. Explain that it is common in Britain for young people to share houses and flats and that one of the main ways of finding someone to share with is via an advertisement in the paper. You might like to discuss some of the pros and cons of this method.

2   Now divide the class into pairs (A and B) and give each students the appropriate handout. Give them a few minutes to read and decide on some questions to ask. Then ask them to sit back to back as though they were making a phone call and allow five minutes for the simulation.

3   After five minutes, stop the activity and ask if they felt able to make a judgement on the phone about whether they would like to share a house together. What other information would they need?

4   Now pass to the second part of the activity – the interview. Ask for (or choose) two students to play the people who are already in the house and three others to be possible house-sharers who have come along to see the house and be interviewed.

These five students come to the front of the class and play out the scene where questions are asked and answered on both sides.

5   While this is going on, give the rest of the class things to listen out for e.g., listen out for any good or not-so-good questions; good or not-so-good replies; possible problems; problems in language and expression, etc.

6   When the role-play is over, ask the class for feedback and end with a vote: which of the three would be offered the place in the house and would they like to live there themselves?

7   Follow-up homework could be to write about the advantages and disadvantages of this kind of living.

50 Hot issues

Time: 30 minutes
Type of activity: Teacher-led discussion
Preparation: Make one copy of page 121 per student

Grammar points
Giving opinions
I think .../In my opinion .../My view is .../
I believe ..., etc.
Agreeing
Yes, I agree./I couldn't agree more./That's a very good point., etc.
Disagreeing
Well, I disagree./That's not right./It's very doubtful., etc.

Method

1 Divide the class into small groups (5–7 students) and give each student a copy of the handout. Read out the following 15 sentences in order. After you have read each one, tell the students to give their opinion by writing a key word in one of the columns 1–10 to express their opinion. If they put the word in column 1, it means they disagree very strongly; if they put the word in column 10, it means they agree very strongly, etc.

2 When you have finished, students will have 15 words on their sheets. Ask one group to give you a number between 1 and 15. When they do so, read out that statement again. The students in the group now show one another where they have placed the word and a short discussion can begin. Encourage them to agree and disagree with one another. Their aim is to try to get others to change their minds. If you think it would be useful, revise ways of giving opinion, agreeing and disagreeing and write examples on the board to encourage students to use a wide range of structures. After two minutes, stop the discussion and ask a group what their opinion is, whether unanimous or divided. Did anyone change their mind as a result of the discussion?

3 Carry on with another number chosen by the next group until all 15 issues have been discussed.

4 As a follow-up, ask each group in turn which statement caused the most discussion.

5 Students could choose one of the issues to write about for homework.

The Fifteen Hot Issues

Read out the following, with the key words if you wish:

1 All genetically-modified food should be banned. (GM Food)

2 The most important thing about a job is the money you earn. (Money)

3 You should look after your parents when they are old, even if this means one or more of your parents living with you. (Parents)

4 Most people in my country are prejudiced towards foreigners, but few will admit to it. (Prejudice)

5 It isn't very important if you make a mistake in English as long as people understand you. (Mistakes)

6 It is acceptable for a man to marry a woman much younger than himself, but not for a woman to do so. (Marry)

7 There need to be strict guidelines for advertising. (Advertising)

8 It is impossible to have a successful career and a successful family life. You have to choose one or the other. (Choose)

9 People suffering from incurable diseases should have the choice of being put painlessly to death. (Death)

10 We should try to cure criminals not punish them. (Criminals)

11 No one nowadays should be allowed to have more than one car or one child. (Only one)

12 Watching violent videos makes young people aggressive. (Videos)

13 Getting married and having children is more important for a woman than a man. (Children)

14 There is no such thing as a just war. (War)

15 Pop singers, filmstars and sportsmen and women don't deserve all the money they earn. (Stars)

51 Taking a group photograph

Time: 30 minutes
Type of activity: Giving and following instructions in groups
Preparation: Make one copy of page 122 per 6 students and cut handout into two

Grammar points
Giving and following instructions
Using the imperative and prepositions of place
Sit here./Move to the left./Put your hand on his shoulder.

Using comparatives
Move closer./Lean more forward.

Method

1 Divide class into groups of six. Each group consists of one photographer and five subjects. Extra students should join groups as the photographer's assistant.

2 Choose one student from each group as the (chief) photographer and give him/her a copy of photo 1. They must not show this to the rest of the group.

3 Now the photographer must arrange the five subjects in the group into exactly the same positions as in the photograph, using only words. There must be no gestures at all.

4 Fix a time-limit for this – about five minutes – and then stop everyone. Walk round the class and judge which group is closest to the photograph. You might like to award points out of 10. Let the subjects look at the photo and discuss what was the most difficult pose to get right.

5 Now everyone is warmed up, the activity can be repeated using the second photo and choosing different photographers.

Note: it would be great to have a polaroid camera for this activity. Then you could take a picture of each group and put them up on the wall beside the original.

52 Reasons and excuses

Time: 30 minutes
Type of activity: Asking and answering in pairs
Preparation: Make one copy of page 123 per pair of students and cut handout into two parts

Grammar points

Giving reasons
That's because .../It's because .../The reason is ...
Using various tenses
It's because I've been dieting./It's because he lost his job./That's because she's going out tonight.

Method

1 Divide the class into pairs (A and B) and give each student the appropriate part of the handout.

2 Explain that they each have six statements that they will read to their partner and six lines to write reasons and excuses for what their partner will read to them. You might like to revise the construction *It's .... That's because ...* .

3 Student A now starts by reading sentences 1–6 and Student B writes down answers. Then they change roles. Circulate while this is going on to give help and encouragement as needed.

4 When they have finished, put small groups (3–5) of Student A together and small groups of Student B. They now compare their answers and choose the most original.

5 Do a whole class feedback by reading out the statements one by one and asking groups to say which answers they chose.

53 Countable or uncountable?

Time: 20–25 minutes
Type of activity: Small group then whole class
Preparation: Make one copy of page 124 per small group of students (3–5)

Cut up into 40 separate items and keep together (e.g., in an envelope)

Shuffle them up so that the two lists are mixed

Grammar point
Countable and uncountable nouns
He gave me lots of good advice./You can never have enough information./She made some very good suggestions.

Method

1 Divide the class into small groups (3–5 students) and give each group a set of the 40 words.

2 Give them time to separate these into two piles – countable and uncountable.

3 When this has been done, ask each group in turn to pick a word and say whether it is countable or uncountable and use it in a sentence. If they are correct, they get a point. If not, they can be challenged by another group who get an extra point. Continue until all the words have been used.

54 What a question!

Time: 25–30 minutes
Type of activity: Discussion in small groups
Preparation: Make one copy of page 125 per small group of students (3–5) and cut up into 20 cards

Grammar points

Speculating using the second conditional
If I could know one thing, I'd like to know about my future.
If my house caught fire, I'd save my photograph albums.
Even if I were able to cheat, I wouldn't do it.
In that situation I would/might ...
Agreeing and disagreeing
I'd rather .../I agree but .../Have you considered ...?

Method

1 Divide the class into small groups (3–5 students) and give each group a set of cards. They place these face downwards on the table in front of them without reading them. Explain that they are all questions that are very difficult to answer and they will need to speculate on what they would do in certain circumstances. If you think it useful, revise the language of speculation, particularly the second conditional e.g., *If I were ..., I would ..../Even if I could ..., I wouldn't ...*, etc. Also revise ways of agreeing and disagreeing politely; ask for suggestions and make a list on the board.

2 Students now take it in turns to pick a card and read it out to the group, saying what they would or wouldn't do in such circumstances. The rest of the group can then agree or disagree. Encourage them to spend about a minute on each one.

3 After twenty minutes stop the activity and ask students which situations gave rise to the most discussion and why.

4 For homework students could write about one or two of the issues raised.

55 The ask and tell game

Time: 25–30 minutes
Type of activity: Board game for small groups
Preparation: For each group (4–5 students) make one copy of pages 126, 127

and 128. If possible, mount the board on stiff card.

Cut out the Ask and Tell cards being careful to keep each set of 35 together

Provide a counter for each player, e.g. coins

Provide a dice for each group

Grammar points

General grammar
Asking a variety of questions
What are you good at?/Which person from history do you admire?
Giving a variety of information
I find it difficult to learn spelling./I went to France last year.

Method

1 Assemble groups of 4–5 students around a table. Give each group a board plus a set of *Ask* cards and a set of *Tell* cards. The cards are placed face down in two piles next to the board. Each group also needs a dice and a different counter for each player.

2 Each player starts in the square marked 'Start'. One student begins by throwing the dice and moving his/her counter the appropriate number of squares. If the counter lands on an *Ask* square, the student picks up an *Ask* card from the top of the pile and asks somebody else in the group that particular question. If on the other hand, the counter lands on a *Tell* square, the student picks up a *Tell* card and must tell the others about the particular item on that card.

3 Play continues in this way until one or more players land in the end square at the top of the board.

4 If the class enjoy this activity, it could be played again in different groups.

56 Keep talking!

Time: 20–25 minutes
Type of activity: Fluency activity for whole class or groups
Preparation: If this is to be a whole class activity, make one copy of page 129

For a group activity, make one copy per group (5–7 students)

Cut up into 12 cards

Grammar points
Asking a wide variety of questions in various tenses
Why don't you like him?/What did you tell her?/Where are you moving to?/Why do you wish that?
Fluency practice

Method

For whole class activity

1 Demonstrate the activity by choosing a card yourself (you can choose which one best suits you!). Read what is on it to the class. Their challenge is now to keep you talking on this subject for three minutes by asking you as many detailed questions as they can. As you give answers, they should be able to think of more questions.

2 Ask for volunteers to come up to the front of the class and continue in the same way with the remaining cards.

For group activity

1 Demonstrate with one card as above.

2 Then divide class into groups (5–7 students) and give each group a set of cards. They work together with each member of the group taking it in turn to say the opening statement and then answer questions. This time you might like to ask them to see how long they can ask questions for on each topic.

3 As a round-up, ask some groups to give an example to the class of their longest question and answer session.

57 What does it mean?

Time: 20 minutes
Type of activity: Teacher-led
Preparation: Make one copy of page 130 per student

Grammar point
Phrasal verbs
put down/get on/cut down, etc.

Method

1 Give each student a copy of the handout.

2 Read out the sentences below and give time for students to write down their answers each time.

3 Check orally.

4 Put students in pairs; ask them to remember what context was given for each phrasal verb and to suggest another situation in which it could be used.

5 Each group then reads out their new situation and the rest of the class give the appropriate phrasal verb. Check and give points if you so wish.

Sentences to read out.

Note that the answer is given each time in brackets.

1 Write the number 1 next to the person who has been attacked.
   (i I've been beaten up.)

2 Write the number 2 next to the person who has just been given a job.
   (m They've decided to take me on.)

3 Write the number 3 next to the person who has quarrelled with someone.
   (p We've fallen out again.)

4 Write the number 4 next to the person who wants something to be kept secret.
   (a Don't let on!)

5 Write the number 5 next to the person who is really tired.
   (h I'm worn out.)

6 Write the number 6 next to the person who might be talking about a pet that has died.
   (n We had to have him put down.)

7 Write the number 7 next to the person who is offering someone a room for the night.
   (c I can put you up.)

8 Write the number 8 next to the person who might be talking about the goods produced at a factory.
   (o We turn out about a thousand a day.)

9 Write the number 9 next to the person who is talking about a racist.
   (b He's always looked down on foreigners.)

10 Write the number 10 next to the person who might be talking about a bus or a train that is late.
    (k *It's been held up.*)

11 Write the number 11 next to the person who might be worried about the number of cigarettes he or she smokes.
    (d *I really must cut down.*)

12 Write the number 12 next to the person who is talking about someone who has fainted.
    (l *She's passed out.*)

13 Write the number 13 next to the person who is talking about his or her age.
    (g *I'm getting on a bit now.*)

14 Write the number 14 next to the person who is talking about the weather.
    (e *I think it's going to clear up.*)

15 Write the number 15 next to the person who is talking about visiting someone.
    (f *I'll call on you tonight.*)

16 Write the number 16 next to the person who probably wishes he or she had a better car.
    (j *It keeps breaking down.*)

58 Finish the sentence

Time: 10–15 minutes per activity
Type of activity: Finishing sentences from cards in groups
Preparation: Make one copy of page 131 per small group of students (4–6)
                    Cut the cards up

Grammar points
Various structures
wish
I wish my parents were .../I wish teachers would ...
Second conditional
If I had, .../If I were ...
Infinitive
I'd like to .../I'm going to ...
should
People should .../Parents should never ...
Superlatives
happiest/saddest
Present perfect

I still haven't ...

Method

Activity 1

1 Give each group (about 4–6 students) a set of cards, which they place face down on the table.

2 Students take it in turns to pick up a card and read out what is written. They then finish the sentence in any way they like. If the rest of the group judge it is grammatically correct and it makes sense, the player keeps the card. If they consider it incorrect, the player does not keep the card. In case of doubt, they should ask you!

3 Play continues until all the cards are finished and the person with the most wins.

4 This game can easily be played again with different groups or if you prefer, different sentences.

Activity 2

1 As before students sit in small groups with a set of cards face down in front of them.

2 One student starts by picking up a card, reading out what is written and finishing the sentence. The person next to them now also finishes the same sentence by giving an alternative ending. This continues until somebody is unable to think of a new ending. That person is then out and play continues until only one person is left. That player keeps the card.

3 The person who was out first now picks another card and play continues in the same way, either for a fixed time or until all cards have been used.

59 Explain yourself!

Time: 25–30 minutes
Type of activity: Teacher-led activity
Preparation: Make one copy of page 132 per class and cut it up into 13 parts

Grammar points
Giving excuses and reasons
Clauses using *because*
Past tenses – simple and continuous

I was chasing the policeman because he had my
identity card.
I left the exam because I lost my contact lenses.

Method

1   Divide the class into small groups (no more than thirteen groups so that each group can have a different card).

2   Give each group a card with a situation on it and allow them five minutes to work together to come up with a logical explanation.

3   Each group now chooses a spokesperson who comes out to the front and gives the explanation. The rest of the class try to find flaws and inconsistencies in this explanation and cross question the speaker, asking as many questions about details as they can. Finally they decide whether or not they accept the explanation and if not, why not.

4   The activity can be repeated with any cards that have not been used or groups could be asked to come up with different logical explanations.

60 Urban myths

Time: 25–30 minutes
Type of activity: Teacher-led memory game
Preparation: Make one copy of page 133 per student

Grammar points
General grammar revision
Answering questions
What happens if ...?/Why is it dangerous to ...?/What's so special about ...?/How can you ...?/Why do ...?
Reading comprehension
Giving information – various tenses
Your phone calls will be free./... by putting them in the freezer./To see how well they can forge notes.

Method

1   Write 'urban myths' on the board and explain what they are i.e., a commonly-believed untrue fact or explanation. Tell them they are now going to learn twelve urban myths and give each person a copy of the handout.

2   Allow them five minutes to read through the urban myths and memorize them. They are not allowed to write anything down.

3   At the end of the time, everyone must turn their papers over and write the numbers 1–12, either on the back of the handout or on a separate piece of paper (as you prefer).

4   Read out the following twelve questions, giving students time to note down their answers.

5   Check orally, asking students to exchange papers so that they mark one another's papers.

6   Finally put students into pairs and see how many of the myths they can remember. You could continue the discussion by asking for possible explanations for the growth of these myths and if they know of any others.

QUESTIONS TO READ OUT

1   What happens if you dial a special, secret telephone number?

2   Why is it dangerous to fall asleep on the London Underground?

3   Why do the Bank of England test all new photocopiers, faxes and laser printers?

4   What had the woman lost? Who found it and where?

5   Where might you find ink made from crushed butterfly wings?

6   If a vicious dog attacks you, how can you protect yourself?

7   What, according to an ancient British law, can you do to legally get another person's money?

8   How can you recharge phone cards?

9   What happens to a hamster if you pick it up by its tail?

10 What sometimes happens on the Tokyo metro?

11 Why have the oil companies paid off some scientists?

12 What's so special about shop mirrors?

SUGGESTED ANSWERS

1   Your phone calls will be free from then on.

2   You might kill yourself.

3   To see how well they can forge notes.

4   Her watch. Her husband. It was inside a fish he had caught.

5   In US dollar bills.

6   By grabbing its front legs and quickly pulling them apart.

7   Guess exactly how much money (s)he is carrying.

8   By putting them in the freezer overnight.

9   Its eyes pop out.

10 People die and travel around for days.

11 Because they have invented a car that runs on water.

12 They make you look slimmer.

Acknowledgement: These facts are taken from *The Return of Urban Myths* by Phil Healey and Richard Glanville, published by Virgin Books, 1993.

Part 2:
Material for photocopying

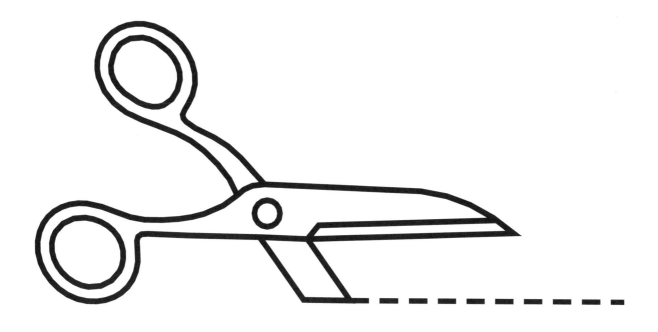

1 Find someone who . . .

Find someone:

1 who thinks he's/she's a good cook.
(Find out his or her 'speciality'.)

_____

2 who belongs to a club or a society.
*(Find out what sort of club or society
it is.)*

_____

3 who collects something as a hobby.
(Find out what.)

_____

4 who reads a newspaper or
magazine regularly.
(Find out which one.)

_____

5 who remembers his or her dreams.
*(Find out what a typical dream is
about.)*

_____

6 who usually goes to bed late.
(Find out what time.)

_____

7 who has a pet.
*(Find out what sort and if it has a
name.)*

_____

8 who watches satellite television.
*(Find out his or her favourite
programme.)*

_____

9 who speaks more than two foreign
languages.
(Find out what they are.)

_____

10 who likes reading books.
(Find out his or her favourite author.)

_____

11 who has a relative who lives
abroad.
(Find out in which country.)

_____

12 who knows a famous person.
(Find out who it is.)

_____

13 who sends a lot of e-mails.
(Find out who s/he sends them to.)

_____

14 who plays a musical instrument.
(Find out what.)

_____

2 Bingo: What's the time? Teacher's board

1:00	1:20	2:05	2:50	3:15	11:15
3:45	4:10	4:35	5:25	5:55	12:40
6:30	6:40	7:00	7:15	8:30	8:05
9:25	9:35	10:00	11:55	12:35	10:50

2 Bingo: What's the time? Teacher's numbers

1:00	1:20	2:05	2:50	3:15	11:15
3:45	4:10	4:35	5:25	5:55	12:40
6:30	6:40	7:00	7:15	8:30	8:05
9:25	9:35	10:00	11:55	12:35	10:50

From *Grammar Games and Activities Book 1* © Penguin Books 2001

2 Bingo: What's the time?

CARD 1

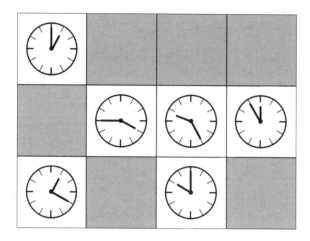

CARD 2

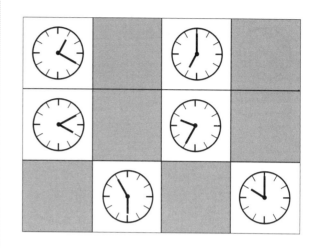

CARD 3

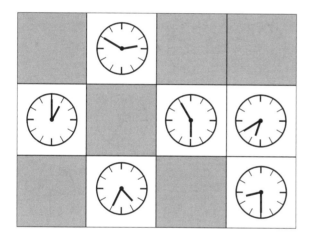

CARD 4

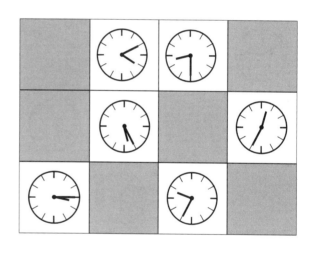

CARD 5

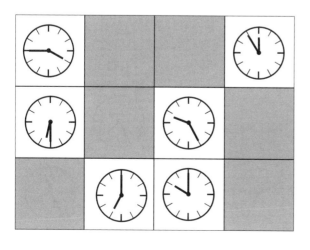

CARD 6

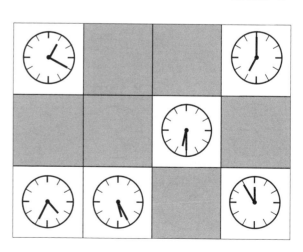

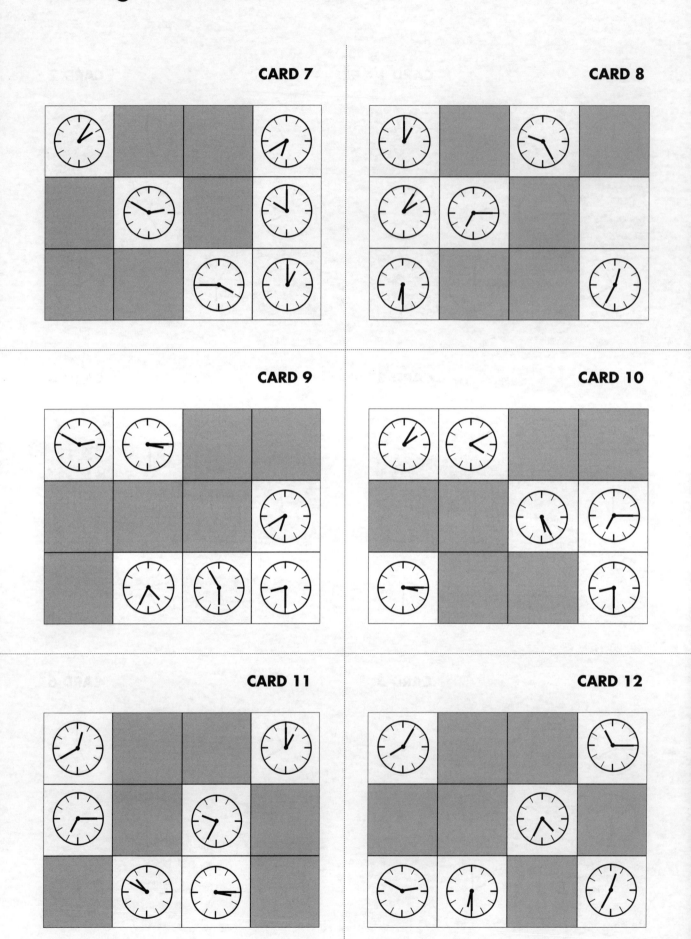

3 Bingo: Telephone numbers   Teacher's board

103231	117720	148720	189480
215088	991340	253865	345578
346445	423518	441005	014996
472552	501447	650381	690931
720305	882117	740540	830451
843230	866035	977420	254502

3 Bingo: Telephone numbers   Teacher's numbers

103231	117720	148720	189480
215088	991340	253865	345578
346445	423518	441005	014996
472552	501447	650381	690931
720305	882117	740540	830451
843230	866035	977420	254502

3 Bingo: Telephone numbers

CARD 1

103231			
	253865	720305	866035
117720		843230	

CARD 2

117720		650381	
345578		830451	
	441005		843230

CARD 3

	189480		
103231		441005	501447
	346445		720305

CARD 4

	345578	740540	
	423518		977420
215088		830451	

CARD 5

253865			977420
472552		830451	
	650381	843230	

CARD 6

117720			650381
		472552	
346445	423518		866035

 From *Grammar Games and Activities Book 1* © Penguin Books 2001

3 Bingo: Telephone numbers   Student's cards 7–12

CARD 7

148720			501447
	189480		843230
		253865	866035

CARD 8

103231		750540	
148720	690931		
472552			977420

CARD 9

991340	215088		
			501447
	346445	441005	720305

CARD 10

148720	345578		
		423518	690931
215088			720305

CARD 11

991340			254502
253865		501447	
	189480	977420	

CARD 12

014996			882117
		866035	
103231	253865		740540

4 What's my uncle's job?

1 Doctor

2 Taxi driver

3 Footballer

4 Tourist guide

5 Shop assistant

6 Dentist

7 Teacher

8 Pilot

9 Soldier

10 Writer

11 Actor

12 Waiter

13 Hairdresser

14 Pop singer

15 Farmer

16 Postman

 From *Grammar Games and Activities Book 1* © Penguin Books 2001

5 What are the missing numbers?   Student A

	A	B	C	D	E	F
1		107		23	172	
2	72		58			1,017
3		156		34		328
4		527	95			66

Take it in turns to ask and answer, e.g. **What's the number in square C1? It's ...**
When you have finished, compare your squares.

5 What are the missing numbers?   Student B

	A	B	C	D	E	F
1	43		828			89
2		444		950	118	
3	1,253		608		0	
4	268			739	217	

Take it in turns to ask and answer, e.g. **What's the number in square F4? It's ...**
When you have finished, compare your squares.

6 Fill in the missing dates

	G	H	I	J	K	L
1	3rd	9th		18th	30th	
2		4th			2nd	
3	15th		11th		24th	
4	1st		22nd			19th

Take it in turns to ask and answer, e.g. **What's the date in square I1? It's the . . .**
When you have finished, compare your squares.

6 Fill in the missing dates

Student B

	G	H	I	J	K	L
1			23rd			13th
2	21st		27th	20th		6th
3		8th		5th		16th
4		10th		7th	12th	

Take it in turns to ask and answer, e.g. **What's the date in square G4? It's the . . .**
When you have finished, compare your squares.

   From *Grammar Games and Activities Book 1* © Penguin Books 2001

7 Four people

Work with a partner. Ask and answer questions to fill in the missing information about the following four people.

Before you start, work out what questions to ask, e.g.

- What is Philippa's date of birth?
- Is Philippa married or single?   etc.

Name: *Philippa*	**Name:** *Kurt*
Date of birth:	Date of birth: *1 June 1973*
Country of origin:	Country of origin:
Marital status: *single*	Marital status:
Number of children: *none*	Number of children:
Home town:	Home town: *Berlin*
Present job: *actress*	Present job:
Interests or hobbies: *music*	Interests or hobbies: *collecting antiques*
Dislikes:	Dislikes: *cold weather, people who snore*
Main ambition: *to win an Oscar*	Main ambition:

Name: Maria	**Name:** Jack
Date of birth:	Date of birth: 31 April 1978
Country of origin: Portugal	Country of origin: New Zealand
Marital status: married	Marital status:
Number of children: 2 boys, 1 girl	Number of children:
Home town:	Home town: Wellington
Present job:	Present job: policeman
Interests or hobbies: keep fit	Interests or hobbies: playing rugby
Dislikes: doing the washing-up, writing letters	Dislikes:
Main ambition:	Main ambition: to visit Europe

When you have finished, compare your tables.

7 Four people

Student B

Work with a partner. Ask and answer questions to fill in the missing information about the following four people.

Before you start, work out what questions to ask, e.g.
- Is Philippa married or single?
- What is one of Kurt's interests or hobbies?   etc.

Name: *Philippa*

Date of birth: *18 February 1980*

Country of origin: *Wales*

Marital status:

Number of children:

Home town: *Swansea*

Present job:

Interests or hobbies: *learning languages*

Dislikes: *housework, getting up early*

Main ambition:

Name: *Kurt*

Date of birth:

Country of origin: *Germany*

Marital status: *married*

Number of children: *1 boy*

Home town:

Present job: *journalist*

Interests or hobbies: *painting*

Dislikes:

Main ambition: *to write a novel*

Name: Maria

Date of birth: 12 August 1969

Country of origin:

Marital status:

Number of children:

Home town: Oporto

Present job: teacher

Interests or hobbies: playing tennis

Dislikes:

Main ambition: to travel to America

Name: Jack

Date of birth:

Country of origin:

Marital status: married

Number of children: 2 girls

Home town:

Present job:

Interests or hobbies: playing golf

Dislikes: people who smoke, going to the to the dentist

Main ambition:

When you have finished, compare your tables.

48   **Photocopiable**   From *Grammar Games and Activities Book 1* © Penguin Books 2001

8 Half a crossword: Irregular verbs   Group A

The crossword below is only half filled in. Group B also has a crossword that is only half filled in. Take it in turns to ask what the missing verbs are.

You can ask, for example, e.g. **What's 7 across?**

When you answer, answer like this: **It's the past tense of** (*bite*).

Here are the verbs that Group B will ask for. Before you start, make sure you know the infinitive (eat, bite, etc.) for each of them.

ate	drank	kept	said	taught
bit	dug	lit	sat	threw
broke	fell	lost	shook	told
brought	forgot	rode	spoke	understood
chose	fought			

8 Half a crossword: Irregular verbs   Group B

The crossword below is only half filled in. Group A also has a crossword that is only half filled in. Take it in turns to ask what the missing verbs are.

You can ask, for example, e.g. **What's 3 across?**

When you answer, answer like this: **It's the past tense of** *(begin).*

Here are the verbs that Group A will ask for. Before you start, make sure you know the infinitive (begin, buy, etc.) for each of them.

begin	gave	lay	ran	slept
bought	grew	led	sang	sold
caught	held	left	shot	thought
drew	hid	met	shrank	went
felt	laid			

Photocopiable   From *Grammar Games and Activities Book 1* © Penguin Books 2001

9 A day in the life of ....

Work with a partner. Ask and answer questions to find the missing information in the following table.

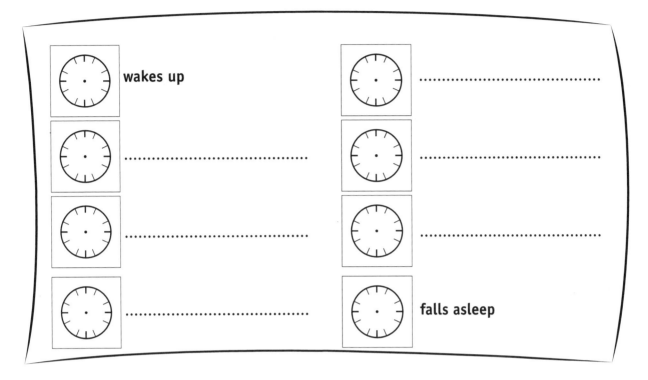

9 A day in the life of ....

Student B

Work with a partner. Ask and answer questions to find the missing information in the following table.

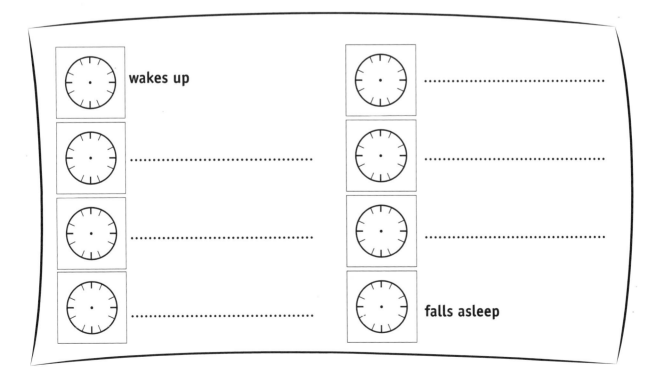

10 Neighbours

Work with a partner. You both have a drawing of a block of flats where you can see people doing different things. But your drawings are not the same.

Ask and answer questions to try to find what is different. You can ask, e.g.

What's the (man, boy, woman, girl, etc.) **doing in flat** (20)?

Are the people in flat (20) (reading a newspaper)?

etc.

When you have finished, compare your drawings.

  From *Grammar Games and Activities Book 1* © Penguin Books 2001

10 Neighbours

Work with a partner. You both have a drawing of a block of flats where you can see people doing different things. But your drawings are not the same.

Ask and answer questions to try to find what is different. You can ask, e.g.

What's the *(man, boy, woman, girl, etc.)* **doing in flat** *(20)***?**

Are the people in flat *(20)* *(reading a newspaper)***?**

etc.

When you have finished, compare your drawings.

11 Up, down, left, right

Read the following out to your partner. He/she is going to draw what you tell him/her to draw. (Don't let him/her see your paper.)

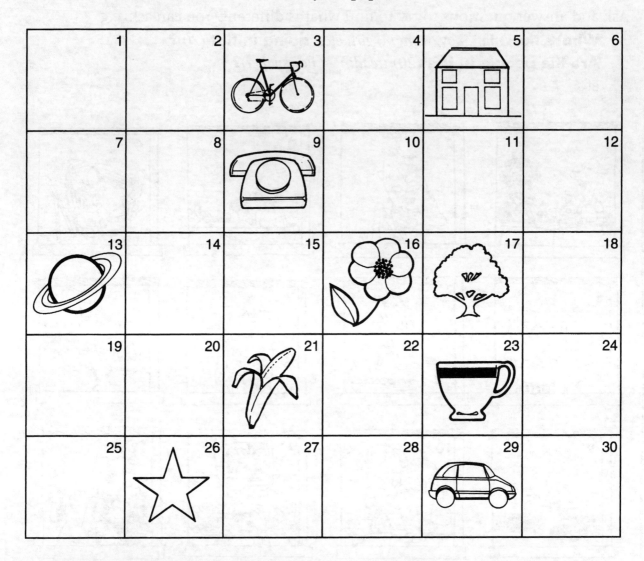

1 Start in the square above the picture of a flower.
2 Go left 2 squares, then down 2 squares. In this square copy the picture in the square below.
3 Go right 4 squares and copy the picture in the square on your left.
4 Go up 2 squares, then left 1 square. In this square copy the picture in the square above.
5 Go left 3 squares then right 2 squares. In this square copy the picture in the square below.
6 Go down 2 squares then left 3 squares. In this square copy the picture in the square above.

Answer

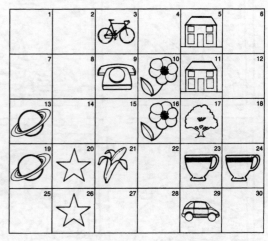

Now check your drawings.
Now it's your turn to listen to instructions. Have a pen or pencil ready. Follow your partner's instructions and draw what he/she tells you to draw. When you have finished, check your drawings.

Photocopiable From *Grammar Games and Activities Book 1* © Penguin Books 2001

11 Up, down, left, right

Have a pen or pencil ready. Follow your partner's instructions and draw what he/she tells you to draw. When you have finished, check your drawings. But hide the bottom part of your paper from Student A.

Now it is your turn to give your partner instructions. Read out the following. He/she is going to draw what you tell him/her to draw.

1 Start in the square below the house.

2 Go down 2 squares, then left 1 square. In this square copy the picture in the square on your left.

3 Go left 2 squares, then up 2 squares. In this square copy the picture in the square on your right.

4 Go down 1 square, then right 4 squares. In this square copy the picture in the square on your left.

5 Go down 1 square, then left 5 squares. In this square, copy the picture in the square above.

6 Go up 3 squares, then right 3 squares. In this square copy the picture in the square on your left.

Now check your drawings.

Answer

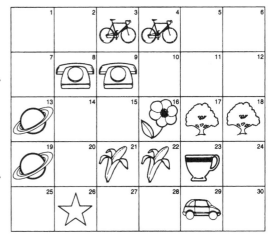

12 A country scene   Student A

12 A country scene   Student B

          From *Grammar Games and Activities Book 1* © Penguin Books 2001

13 Do you know me well?

Student A

Your partner:

	True	False	Correct?
1 enjoys using the Internet.	☐	☐	☐
2 likes going to parties.	☐	☐	☐
3 doesn't often lose his/her temper.	☐	☐	☐
4 is romantic.	☐	☐	☐
5 thinks fashion is a waste of money.	☐	☐	☐
6 wants a big family.	☐	☐	☐
7 prefers pop music to classical music.	☐	☐	☐
8 can sing a song in English.	☐	☐	☐
9 has a mobile phone.	☐	☐	☐
10 eats more fish than meat.	☐	☐	☐
11 knows how to play volleyball.	☐	☐	☐
12 isn't afraid of mice.	☐	☐	☐

13 Do you know me well?

Student B

Your partner:

	True	False	Correct?
1 enjoys going to discos.	☐	☐	☐
2 likes learning foreign languages.	☐	☐	☐
3 doesn't often go to the cinema.	☐	☐	☐
4 is not very good with money.	☐	☐	☐
5 watches too much television.	☐	☐	☐
6 wants to be very rich one day.	☐	☐	☐
7 prefers football to tennis.	☐	☐	☐
8 can play a musical instrument.	☐	☐	☐
9 has a cat.	☐	☐	☐
10 does not eat meat.	☐	☐	☐
11 sends a lot of e-mails.	☐	☐	☐
12 isn't afraid of snakes.	☐	☐	☐

14 Can you follow instructions?

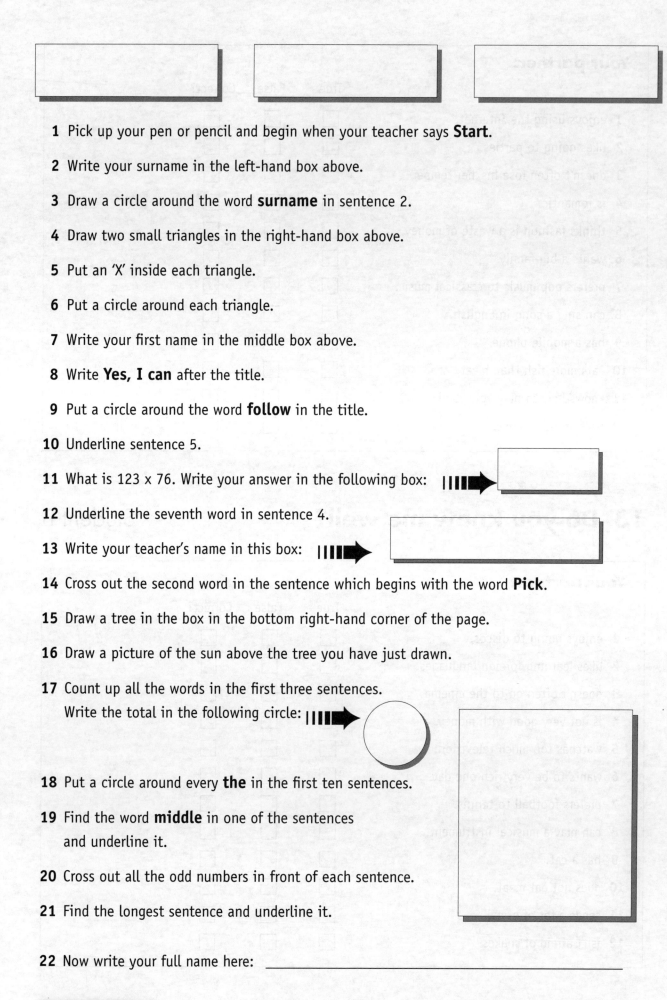

1 Pick up your pen or pencil and begin when your teacher says **Start**.

2 Write your surname in the left-hand box above.

3 Draw a circle around the word **surname** in sentence 2.

4 Draw two small triangles in the right-hand box above.

5 Put an 'X' inside each triangle.

6 Put a circle around each triangle.

7 Write your first name in the middle box above.

8 Write **Yes, I can** after the title.

9 Put a circle around the word **follow** in the title.

10 Underline sentence 5.

11 What is 123 x 76. Write your answer in the following box:

12 Underline the seventh word in sentence 4.

13 Write your teacher's name in this box:

14 Cross out the second word in the sentence which begins with the word **Pick**.

15 Draw a tree in the box in the bottom right-hand corner of the page.

16 Draw a picture of the sun above the tree you have just drawn.

17 Count up all the words in the first three sentences.
Write the total in the following circle:

18 Put a circle around every **the** in the first ten sentences.

19 Find the word **middle** in one of the sentences
and underline it.

20 Cross out all the odd numbers in front of each sentence.

21 Find the longest sentence and underline it.

22 Now write your full name here: _____

          From *Grammar Games and Activities Book 1* © Penguin Books 2001

15 Make a sentence – score a point!   Verb sheet 1

1 begin	**2** break	**3** buy	**4** drink
5 drive	**6** eat	**7** fall	**8** feel
9 find	**10** fly	**11** forget	**12** give
13 go	**14** know	**15** learn	**16** leave

1	**2**	**3**	**4**
lose	make	meet	pay
5	**6**	**7**	**8**
sell	send	shoot	sing
9	**10**	**11**	**12**
speak	spend	stand	swim
13	**14**	**15**	**16**
teach	think	win	write

   From *Grammar Games and Activities Book 1* © Penguin Books 2001

1	2	3	4
5	6	7	8
9	10	11	12
13	14	15	16

16 I like this but I don't like that!

pop music   **go to the dentist**   **1**

Find out: 1 who likes singing in the shower.   *Name* _____

2 who doesn't like meat.   *Name* _____

Indian food   **fly**   **2**

Find out: 1 who loves watching late-night
movies on television.   *Name* _____

2 who doesn't like cats.   *Name* _____

sing in the shower   **the smell of cigarettes**   **3**

Find out: 1 who likes pop music.   *Name* _____

2 who doesn't like opera.   *Name* _____

the smell of fresh coffee   **cats**   **4**

Find out: 1 who likes Indian food.   *Name* _____

2 who hates the smell of fish.   *Name* _____

          From *Grammar Games and Activities Book 1* © Penguin Books 2001

16 I like this but I don't like that!

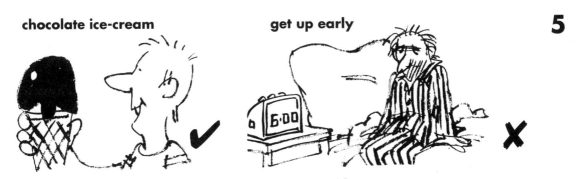

chocolate ice-cream   **get up early**   **5**

Find out: 1 who loves the smell of fresh coffee. *Name* _____

2 who doesn't like going to the dentist. *Name* _____

learn English   **opera**   **6**

Find out: 1 who likes going to parties. *Name* _____

2 who hates flying. *Name* _____

go to parties   **meat**   **7**

Find out: 1 who likes chocolate ice-cream. *Name* _____

2 who hates the smell of cigarettes. *Name* _____

watch late-night movies on television   **the smell of fish**   **8**

Find out: 1 who likes learning English. *Name* _____

2 who hates getting up early. *Name* _____

17 A family tree

Work in a group of six. Each of you has some information about the James family. Working together, fill in the missing names in the family tree and also the jobs of the people in the middle row. You are only allowed to read out – not show – the pieces of information you have.

The James Family Tree

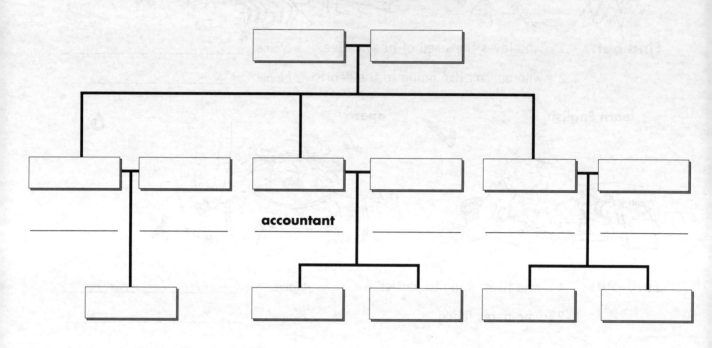

accountant

1 Tom's grandfather is called Douglas.	1 Amanda's mother is a nurse.
2 Sally's husband is an electrician.	2 Peter has two daughters.
3 Anne has two boys.	3 Sylvia's daughter-in-law is a doctor.
4 Rebecca is Amanda's cousin.	4 David and Peter are brothers.
1 The editor is married to David.	1 Sally is Bob's aunt.
2 Mark is Amanda's father.	2 One of Peter's nephews is called Bob.
3 Joanna and Rebecca are sisters.	3 David married Anne.
4 Douglas has two sons and a daughter.	4 Amanda is an only child.
1 Joanna's father is a teacher.	1 Peter is Sylvia's son.
2 Sylvia is a grandmother.	2 Sally has two brothers.
3 Nina is Peter's wife.	3 The accountant is called David.
4 Mark is Sylvia's son-in-law.	4 Bob and Tom are brothers.

Photocopiable *From Grammar Games and Activities Book 1* © Penguin Books 2001

18 Left, right, up, down

Fill in the following on your answer sheet.

> **1** In square number 2, write tomorrow's date.
>
> **2** In square number 4, write your first name.
>
> **3** In square number 6, write what year it is.
>
> **4** In square number 8, write the colour of your shoes.
>
> **5** In square number 14, write the number 7,537.
>
> **6** In square number 17, write the name of the capital of Japan.
>
> **7** In square number 23, write your teacher's surname.
>
> **8** In square number 25, write what day it is today.

Now read the following instructions to your partner. Do not let him/her see your answer sheet.

1 Start in the square below the black square. Go right 2 squares then up 1 square. Draw a picture of a lamp in this square.

2 Go down 3 squares, then right 1 square. Write which day it is today in this square.

3 Go left 3 squares. Draw a picture of an apple in this square, and in the square on your right your teacher's surname.

4 Go back to the black square. Go up 1 square and write tomorrow's date. Then, in the square on your left draw a comb and in the square on your right draw a triangle.

5 Go to the square to the right of the apple. Go up 2 squares, then right 1 square. Write the number 7,537 in this square.

6 Go left 3 squares and draw a picture of a pair of scissors and in the square below this a picture of a clock.

7 Go to the square in the top right-hand corner and draw a picture of a candle.

8 Go down 3 squares, then left 3 squares. In this square write the name of the capital of Japan.

9 Go up 2 squares, then left 1 square. In this square write what year it is.

10 Go to the square under the candle. Go left 2 squares, then down 1 square. Draw a picture of a fish in this square and in the square above write the colour of my shoes.

11 Go to the square in the bottom left-hand corner. Go right 3 squares. Draw a picture of a cross in this square.

12 Go up 4 squares and write my first name in this square.

13 Finally, go right 1 square, go down 2 squares, go left 3 squares, go down 1 square again and then go right 3 squares. In this square draw a picture of a chair.

When you have finished, compare grids.

1	**2**	**3**	**4**	**5**
6	**7**	**8**	**9**	**10**
11	**12**	**13**	**14**	**15**
16	**17**	**18**	**19**	**20**
21	**22**	**23**	**24**	**25**

From *Grammar Games and Activities Book 1* © Penguin Books 2001

18 Left, right, up, down

Here is a grid with 25 squares. You are going to write or draw something in 18 of them. Your partner will tell you what to write or draw. You are allowed to ask your partner questions, but you must not ask him/her for the number of the square you are to write or draw in.

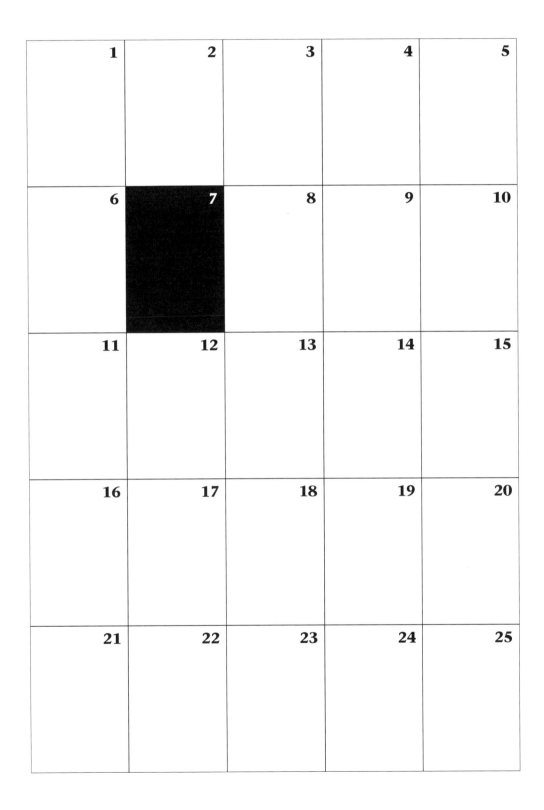

When you have finished, compare grids to see if you filled in everything correctly.

From *Grammar Games and Activities Book 1* © Penguin Books 2001 **Photocopiable** 67

19 True or false?

Is it true or false that:

		True	False
1	more than three people in the group have visited Rome?	☐	☐
2	at least four people watched the news on TV last night?	☐	☐
3	no one was born in June?	☐	☐
4	more than two people are going out tonight?	☐	☐
5	more than half the group have a mobile phone?	☐	☐
6	at least two people are vegetarians?	☐	☐
7	only one person likes getting up early?	☐	☐
8	someone in the group knows somebody famous?	☐	☐
9	most of the group have had a cold this year?	☐	☐
10	the average height of the people in this group is over 1 metre 75?	☐	☐

Use these boxes to fill in names/details, etc.

Q1	**Q6**
Q2	**Q7**
Q3	**Q8**
Q4	**Q9**
Q5	**Q10**

From *Grammar Games and Activities Book 1* © Penguin Books 2001

20 Find the differences

Student A

Work with a partner. You both have a drawing but your drawings are not the same.
Ask and answer questions to find out what is different. Only answer the questions
your partner asks. Do not give any extra information. Put a circle around any
differences you find. You can ask, e.g.

How many people are there in the room?
Are there any paintings on the wall?
Is the *(man, woman, dog, etc.)* **reading a newspaper?**

etc.

When you have finished, compare your drawings.

Work with a partner. You both have a drawing but your drawings are not the same.
Ask and answer questions to find out what is different. Only answer the questions
your partner asks. Do not give any extra information. Put a circle around any
differences you find. You can ask, e.g.

How many people are there in the room?
Are there any paintings on the wall?
Is the *(man, woman, dog, etc.)* **reading a newspaper?**

etc.

When you have finished, compare your drawings.

From *Grammar Games and Activities Book 1* © Penguin Books 2001

21 What did you do last week?

You went to a party last Tuesday. It was your cousin's birthday. She was 18.　　　**1**

Others in the class:

1　went to Brighton last Wednesday.
　Find out who they went to see.

2　saw the film *Tarzan meets James Bond* last week.
　Find out when they went to see it.

3　bought a second-hand car for £4,000 last week.
　Find out what sort of car they bought.

You bought a car last Sunday – a white second-hand Volvo. You paid £4,000 for it.　　　**2**

Others in the class:

1　went to the cinema last weekend.
　Find out what they thought of the film.

2　went to their uncle's birthday party last week.
　Find out which day that was.

3　went to Brighton last Wednesday.
　Find out how they got there.

You went to the cinema last Saturday. You saw the film *Tarzan meets James Bond*. It was a very good film.　　　**3**

Others in the class:

1　went to a party last Tuesday.
　Find out whose party it was.

2　went to Brighton by car last week.
　Find out when they went there.

3　bought a red car last week.
　Find out what sort of car they bought.

You went to Brighton last Wednesday to see your grandmother. You went there by train.　　　**4**

Others in the class:

1　bought a Volvo last weekend.
　Find out if it was new or second-hand.

2　went to their cousin's birthday party last week.
　Find out on which day it was.

3　saw a terrible film at the cinema last week.
　Find out what it was called.

21 What did you do last week?

You went to a party last Saturday. It was your uncle's birthday. He was 50.   **5**

Others in the class:

1 bought a car last Sunday.
   Find out how much they paid for it.

2 saw the film *The Last Cowboy* last week.
   Find out when they went to see it.

3 went to Brighton last Thursday.
   Find out how they got there.

You bought a car last Saturday – a brand-new Ford. It was red.   **6**

Others in the class:

1 went to a party last Saturday.
   Find out whose party it was.

2 went to Brighton by train last week.
   Find out when they went there.

3 saw a good film at the cinema last week.
   Find out what the film was called.

You went to the cinema last Tuesday. You saw the film *The Last Cowboy*. It was terrible.   **7**

Others in the class:

1 went to Brighton last Thursday.
   Find out who they went to see.

2 bought a Ford car last week.
   Find out on which day they bought it.

3 went to their cousin's birthday party last week.
   Find out how old the cousin was.

You went to Brighton last Thursday to see some friends. You went there by car.   **8**

Others in the class:

1 went to the cinema last Tuesday.
   Find out what they thought of the film.

2 bought a new car last weekend.
   Find out what colour it was.

3 went to their uncle's birthday party last week.
   Find out how old the uncle was.

Photocopiable   From *Grammar Games and Activities Book 1* © Penguin Books 2001

22 Do you have a good memory?

Look at this drawing for three minutes. You are not allowed to write anything down.

When your teacher tells you to stop, turn your drawing over, then write down the answers to the questions you will be asked on a separate piece of paper. Number them 1–15.

Work with a partner. Ask and answer questions to find the missing information in the following short biographies of Picasso and David Livingstone. For example:

When was Picasso born?

Why did David Livingstone go to Africa?

etc.

Who was Picasso?

Picasso was born in 18 _____ in _____, Spain. When he started work, the great painters of the Impressionist movement were still alive. His early pictures – done mainly in blue – showed the _____ he saw around him in Barcelona.

Later he moved to Paris where he worked with Georges _____ on pictures showing figures as fragments of geometric shapes – the style we know as _____.

He became more deeply involved with politics, especially during the Spanish Civil War. One of Picasso's most famous paintings is *Guernica*, which depicts _____. Picasso died in the south of France in 1973.

Who was David Livingstone?

David Livingstone was born in 1813. He went to Africa in 1841, to _____ _____ and to teach Christianity to the Africans.

Livingstone made several journeys on foot into _____. He saw the Kalahari Desert and followed the River Zambezi to discover the magnificent _____. He was horrified by _____ and did all he could to stop it.

In 1866 Livingstone set off to search for the source of the River Nile. Nothing was heard of him until in _____ an expedition led by _____ found him near Lake Tanganyika. Though ill, Livingstone went on exploring until he died, in _____. Two Africans carried his body over 2,000 kilometres to the coast, and returned it to Britain.

When you have finished, compare your biographies.

 From *Grammar Games and Activities Book 1* © Penguin Books 2001

23 Biographies

Work with a partner. Ask and answer questions to find the missing information in the following short biographies of Picasso and David Livingstone. For example:

Where did Picasso move to?

When was David Livingstone born?

etc.

Who was Picasso?

Picasso was born in 1881 in Malaga, Spain. When he started work, the great painters of the _____ movement were still alive. His early pictures – done mainly in _____ – showed the poverty he saw around him in Barcelona.

Later he moved to _____ where he worked with Georges Braque on pictures showing figures as fragments of geometric shapes – the styles we know as cubism.

He became more deeply involved with_____ , especially during the _____War. One of Picasso's most famous paintings is *Guernica*, which depicts the destruction of a Spanish town. Picasso died in _____ in 1973.

Who was David Livingstone?

David Livingstone was born in _____. He went to _____ in 1841, to practise medicine and to teach Christianity to the Africans.

Livingstone made several journeys on foot into the unknown heart of Africa. He saw the Kalahari Desert and followed the River _____ to discover the magnificent Victoria Falls. He was horrified by the slave trade and did all he could to stop it.

In 1866 Livingstone set off to search for _____. Nothing was heard of him until in 1871 an expedition led by Henry Morton Stanley found him near _____ . Though ill, Livingstone went on exploring until he died, in 1873. Two Africans carried his body _____ kilometres to the coast, and returned it to Britain.

When you have finished, compare your biographies.

24 Life style surveys

Interview six other people in the class about **sport** and write down their answers. (People may also ask you questions.)

Do you:	1	2	3	4	5	6
play football or any other team sport?						
go out and watch sport live?						
do any individual sports, e.g. running or swimming?						
follow the Olympic Games on TV?						
try to keep fit?						

Answer Key
1 = Yes, always **2** = Yes, usually **3** = Yes, sometimes
4 = No, not usually **5** = No, hardly ever **6** = No, never

1

Interview six other people in the class about **free time and entertainment** and write down their answers. (People may also ask you questions.)

Do you:	1	2	3	4	5	6
go out in the evenings?						
have many parties at home?						
go to the cinema?						
go dancing?						
spend the weekend with friends?						

Answer Key
1 = Yes, always **2** = Yes, usually **3** = Yes, sometimes
4 = No, not usually **5** = No, hardly ever **6** = No, never

2

Interview six other people in the class about **travel and holidays** and write down their answers. (People may also ask you questions.)

Do you:	1	2	3	4	5	6
use public transport?						
travel more than 5 kilometres a day?						
sunbathe a lot on holiday?						
have a skiing holiday in the winter?						
spend your summer holidays in your own country?						

Answer Key
1 = Yes, always **2** = Yes, usually **3** = Yes, sometimes
4 = No, not usually **5** = No, hardly ever **6** = No, never

3

Photocopiable

24 Life style surveys

Interview six other people in the class about **food and drink** and write down their answers. (People may also ask you questions.)

Do you:	1	2	3	4	5	6
have three meals a day?						
go to a canteen or restaurant for lunch?						
have a big breakfast?						
enjoy cooking?						
eat a lot of fast food?						

Answer Key
1 = Yes, always   **2** = Yes, usually   **3** = Yes, sometimes
4 = No, not usually   **5** = No, hardly ever   **6** = No, never

4

Interview six other people in the class about **health** and write down their answers. (People may also ask you questions.)

Do you:	1	2	3	4	5	6
take vitamin pills?						
do some form of physical exercise at least once a week?						
sleep at least seven hours every night?						
catch a cold in the winter?						
eat lots of fruit and vegetables?						

Answer Key
1 = Yes, always   **2** = Yes, usually   **3** = Yes, sometimes
4 = No, not usually   **5** = No, hardly ever   **6** = No, never

5

Interview six other people in the class about **shopping** and write down their answers. (People may also ask you questions.)

Do you:	1	2	3	4	5	6
buy your food at the supermarket?						
make a list when you go shopping?						
buy clothes more than once a month?						
wait for the sales before you buy clothes?						
enjoy shopping?						

Answer Key
1 = Yes, always   **2** = Yes, usually   **3** = Yes, sometimes
4 = No, not usually   **5** = No, hardly ever   **6** = No, never

6

25 Find someone who . . .

Find someone:

1 who has been abroad more than five times.
(Find out the first foreign country he or she visited.)

_____

_____

2 who has had a holiday job.
(Find out where he or she worked and what he or she did there.)

_____

_____

3 who has ever read a book by Graham Greene.
(Find out what it was called and what he or she thought of it.)

_____

_____

4 who has been to London.
(Find out what they liked most and hated most about it.)

_____

_____

5 who has lived at his/her present address for more than six years.
(Find out when he or she moved there.)

_____

_____

6 who has done something for charity.
(Find out what he or she did and how much money was raised.)

_____

_____

7 who has been on a diet.
(Find out what sort of diet and how much weight he or she lost.)

_____

_____

8 who has always wanted to be famous.
(Find out who his or her idol was when he or she was a teenager.)

_____

_____

9 who has had more than three different pets.
(Find out what his or her pets were and what he or she called them.)

_____

_____

10 who has looked after a baby.
(Ask him or her to mime what he or she did.)

_____

_____

11 who has been frightened or moved to tears by a film.
(Find out which film and why it was so frightening or moving.)

_____

_____

12 who has seen a ghost or a flying saucer.
(Find out when and what happened.)

_____

_____

From *Grammar Games and Activities Book 1* © Penguin Books 2001

26 Conjunctions bingo

Card 1

1 We still went to the beach _____ the sun wasn't shining.

2 We decided to go home _____ it was getting very late.

3 I phoned her _____ I found her telephone number.

4 I'll lend you the money _____ you pay me back soon.

5 I wouldn't marry him _____ he was the last man on Earth!

Card 2

1 He got the sack _____ he kept turning up late for work.

2 _____ he'd asked me I wouldn't have gone. I hate opera!

3 She'll be very attractive _____ she's lost all that weight.

4 We'll go to the beach _____ the weather stays fine.

5 She arrived early _____ she could help me prepare the meal.

Card 3

1 She was late for work _____ her car broke down.

2 He bought it _____ it was more than he could really afford.

3 Take an umbrella with you _____ it rains.

4 Beethoven composed great music _____ being deaf.

5 You'll be able to play the guitar _____ you have a few lessons.

Card 4

1 She was so upset _____ she burst into tears.

2 I won't come _____ David and Peter come too.

3 We waited patiently _____ the taxi arrived.

4 _____ you do, James, don't mention the party. It's a secret.

5 Some people like classical music _____ others prefer pop music.

Card 5

1 I'll lend you my car _____ you fill it up with petrol.

2 He put on his glasses _____ he could see the board better.

3 The film was so boring _____ I fell asleep.

4 The company will go bankrupt _____ we get a big order soon.

5 She was very happy _____ she met Robert Baker.

Card 6

1 _____ she was very bored, she tried to look interested.

2 There was a loud explosion _____ the bomb went off.

3 We'll book a holiday _____ the new brochure arrives.

4 I'll babysit for you _____ you're back by midnight.

5 I'll take some sandwiches with me _____ I get hungry.

26 Conjunctions bingo

Card 7

1 Try to be nice to her _____ you think of her in private.

2 I was just getting into the bath _____ the phone rang.

3 I don't care _____ she comes to the party or not.

4 Many people throw away clothes _____ others have nothing to wear.

5 She didn't send for the doctor _____ she was feeling really ill.

Card 8

1 He couldn't come to the reunion _____ he was abroad at the time.

2 She married him _____ she didn't really love him.

3 _____ his age, he was still a very good tennis player.

4 We'll go for a picnic _____ it doesn't rain.

5 We used to get punished _____ we arrived late for school.

Card 9

1 There was an unexpected hush _____ the Queen entered the hall.

2 We'll leave _____ John and Pat get here.

3 He carried on playing _____ his knee was hurting him.

4 I took my Visa card with me _____ I bought something.

5 The Beatles wrote wonderful songs _____ not being able to read music.

Card 10

1 You can't leave the table _____ you've eaten all your food!

2 He was standing at the bus stop _____ the accident happened.

3 She used to cry _____ she heard the song her ex-husband used to sing to her.

4 It doesn't bother me _____ we go out tonight or not.

5 _____ I was visiting Brighton, I decided to call on an old friend.

26 Conjunctions bingo
Teacher's words

although	as	as soon as	as long as	because
even if	even though	in case	in spite of	once
provided that	so that	that	unless	until
whatever	when	whenever	whether	while

   From *Grammar Games and Activities Book 1* © Penguin Books 2001

27 Where are the carrots?

You each have some information about the position of the different fruit and vegetables on this stall. Read out your information to your group, but do not show them. Work together to fill in the names and answer the question: **Where are the carrots?**

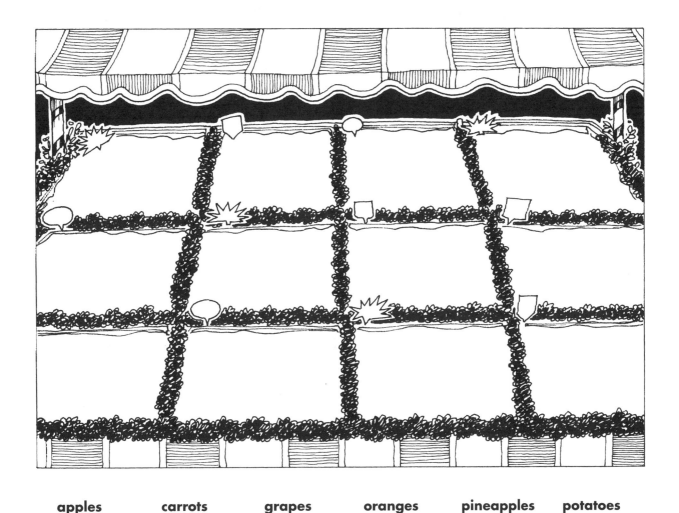

apples	carrots	grapes	oranges	pineapples	potatoes
cabbage	cucumbers	lettuce	peaches	plums	sprouts

1 No two fruits or vegetables are directly next to each other.
2 The cucumbers are on the left of the grapes.
3 The potatoes are in the bottom right corner.

1 No two fruits or vegetables are directly above or below each other.
2 The cucumbers are in the bottom row.
3 The plums are in the same column as the peaches.

1 The plums are above the cabbage.
2 The apples are between the lettuce and the sprouts.
3 The potatoes are in the same column as the sprouts.

1 The oranges are above the cucumbers.
2 The sprouts are above the pineapples.
3 The cucumbers are on the right of the peaches.

28 Four people's diaries

You and your partner have a copy of four people's diaries but some of the things marked in them are not the same. Take it in turns to ask and answer questions to try to find out which things are different and put a circle round them in your diaries. Only answer questions you are asked and do not give your partner any extra information.

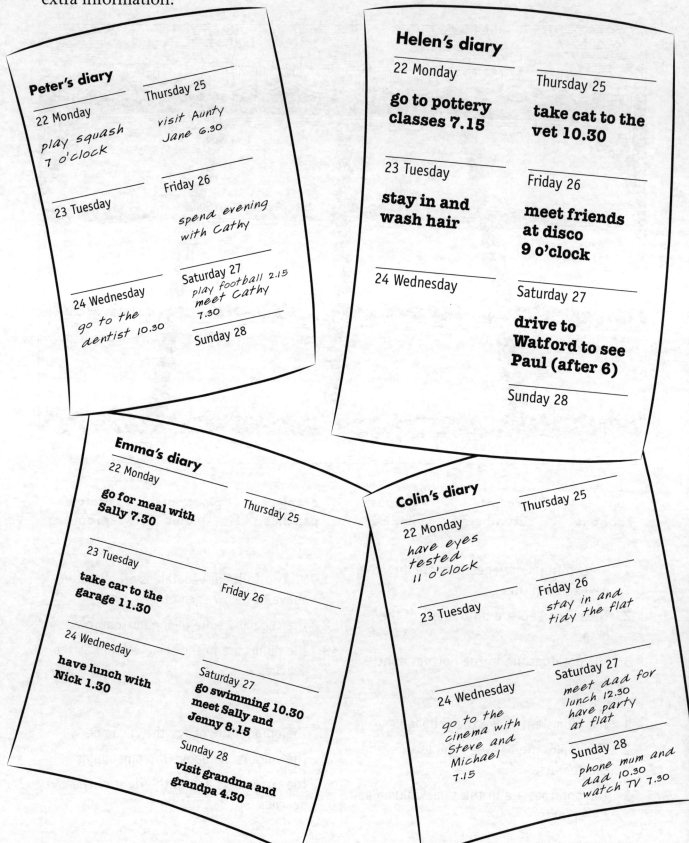

Peter's diary

22 Monday
play squash 7 o'clock

23 Tuesday

24 Wednesday
go to the dentist 10.30

Thursday 25
visit Aunty Jane 6.30

Friday 26
spend evening with Cathy

Saturday 27
play football 2.15 meet Cathy 7.30

Sunday 28

Helen's diary

22 Monday
go to pottery classes 7.15

23 Tuesday
stay in and wash hair

24 Wednesday

Thursday 25
take cat to the vet 10.30

Friday 26
meet friends at disco 9 o'clock

Saturday 27
drive to Watford to see Paul (after 6)

Sunday 28

Emma's diary

22 Monday
go for meal with Sally 7.30

23 Tuesday
take car to the garage 11.30

24 Wednesday
have lunch with Nick 1.30

Thursday 25

Friday 26

Saturday 27
go swimming 10.30 meet Sally and Jenny 8.15

Sunday 28
visit grandma and grandpa 4.30

Colin's diary

22 Monday
have eyes tested 11 o'clock

23 Tuesday

24 Wednesday
go to the cinema with Steve and Michael 7.15

Thursday 25

Friday 26
stay in and tidy the flat

Saturday 27
meet dad for lunch 12.30 have party at flat

Sunday 28
phone mum and dad 10.30 watch TV 7.30

From *Grammar Games and Activities Book 1* © Penguin Books 2001

28 Four people's diaries

You and your partner have a copy of four people's diaries but some of the things marked in them are not the same. Take it in turns to ask and answer questions to try to find out which things are different and put a circle round them in your diaries. Only answer questions you are asked and do not give your partner any extra information.

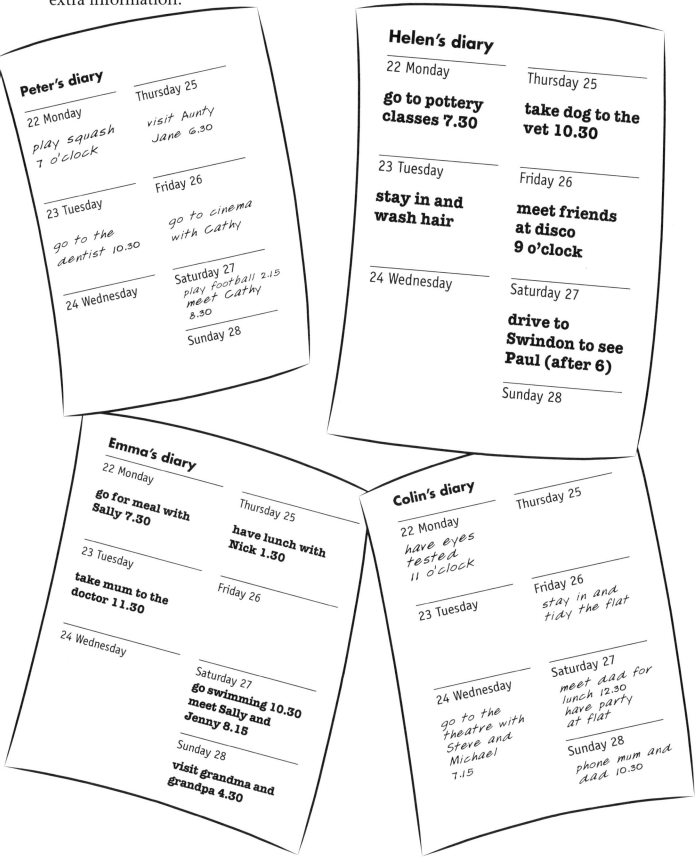

Peter's diary

22 Monday
play squash
7 o'clock

23 Tuesday
go to the
dentist 10.30

24 Wednesday

Thursday 25
visit Aunty
Jane 6.30

Friday 26
go to cinema
with Cathy

Saturday 27
play football 2.15
meet Cathy
8.30

Sunday 28

Helen's diary

22 Monday
go to pottery classes 7.30

23 Tuesday
stay in and wash hair

24 Wednesday

Thursday 25
take dog to the vet 10.30

Friday 26
meet friends at disco 9 o'clock

Saturday 27
drive to Swindon to see Paul (after 6)

Sunday 28

Emma's diary

22 Monday
go for meal with Sally 7.30

23 Tuesday
take mum to the doctor 11.30

24 Wednesday

Thursday 25
have lunch with Nick 1.30

Friday 26

Saturday 27
go swimming 10.30 meet Sally and Jenny 8.15

Sunday 28
visit grandma and grandpa 4.30

Colin's diary

22 Monday
have eyes
tested
11 o'clock

23 Tuesday

24 Wednesday
go to the
theatre with
Steve and
Michael
7.15

Thursday 25

Friday 26
stay in and
tidy the flat

Saturday 27
meet dad for
lunch 12.30
have party
at flat

Sunday 28
phone mum and
dad 10.30

29 Trace the route

On the map below is a route which starts from the station and ends at the library. Your partner has a blank map. Help him/her to trace the same route as yours. You are not allowed to show him/her your map or to point at anything on his/hers.

When you have finished, compare maps.

 From *Grammar Games and Activities Book 1* © Penguin Books 2001

Your partner is going to ask you to trace a route which starts at the station and ends somewhere else. Have a pencil ready to mark the route and write down the name of the building you finish at. You can ask your partner questions but you are not allowed to look at his/her map.

When you have finished, compare maps.

STATION

30 Group opinions

Find out how many in the group:

	1	2	3	4	5	6	7	8
don't trust politicians.								
would rather get an e-mail than a phone call.								
have never broken the law.								
are allergic to something.								
wish they were ten years younger.								
feel all genetically-modified food should be banned.								
believe killing animals is wrong.								
think war can never be justified.								
never borrow money from other people.								
get depressed in the winter.								
worry about what they look like.								
think the internet should be controlled by international law.								

Results

All of us _____

Most of us _____

Many of us _____

Some of us _____

A few of us _____

Not many of us _____

Hardly any of us _____

None of us _____

 From *Grammar Games and Activities Book 1* © Penguin Books 2001

31 Arrange the furniture

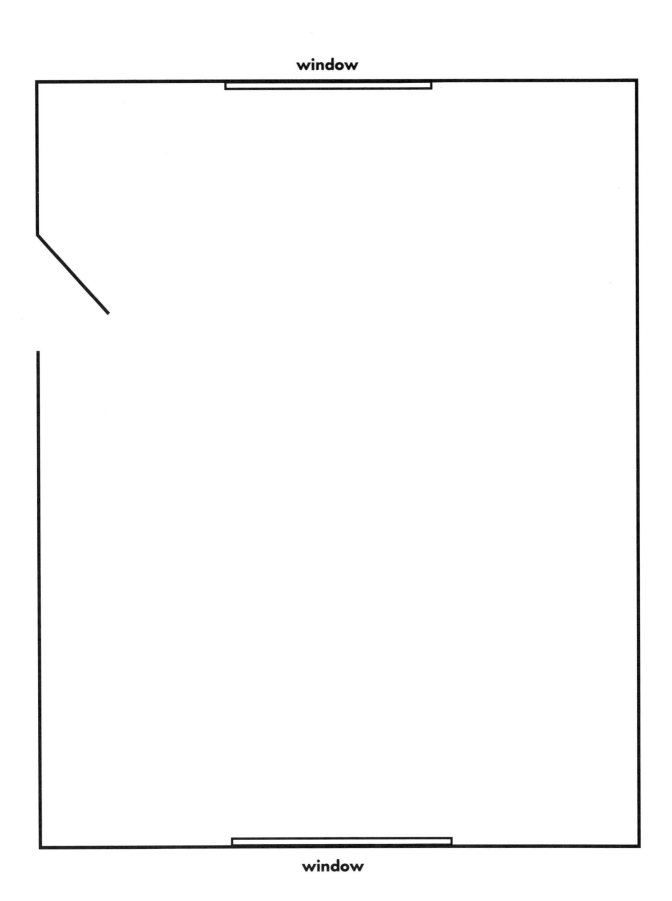

window

window

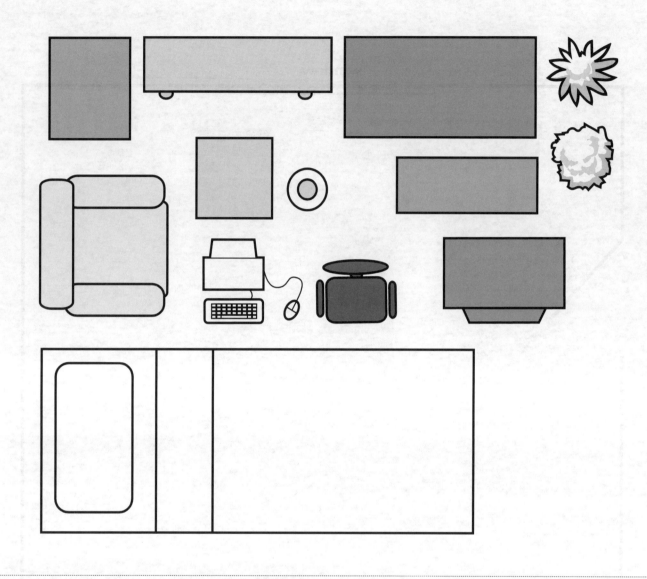

31 Arrange the furniture

Key

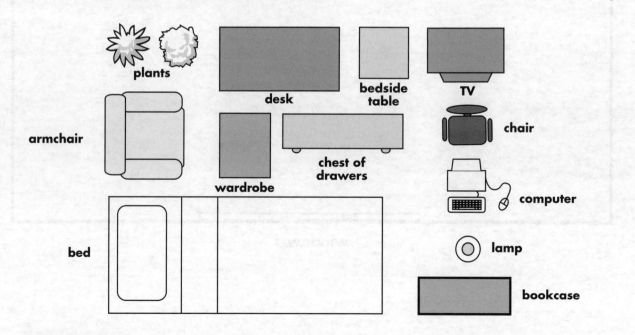

plants

desk

bedside
table

TV

armchair

chair

wardrobe

chest of
drawers

computer

bed

lamp

bookcase

From *Grammar Games and Activities Book 1* © Penguin Books 2001

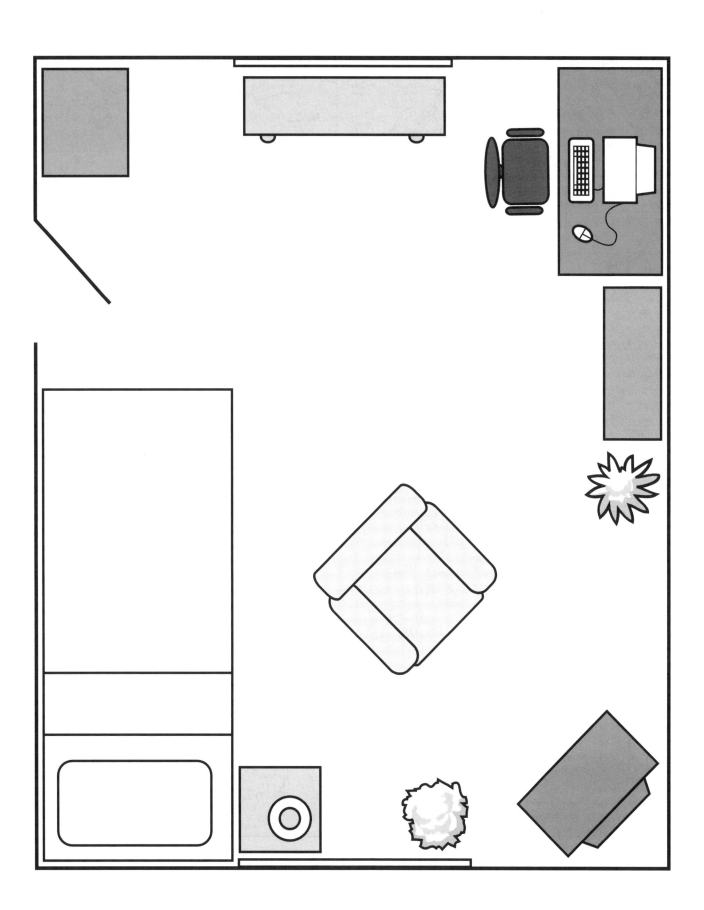

32 What do they have in common?

_____
_____
_____
_____

_____
_____
_____
_____

_____
_____
_____
_____
_____

_____
_____
_____
_____
_____

From *Grammar Games and Activities Book 1* © Penguin Books 2001

33 Prepositions bingo

Card 1

1 Tell me something _____ yourself.
2 I'll see you _____ 8 o'clock.
3 Shall we go out _____ Friday?
4 He was born _____ September.
5 We swam _____ the river to the other side.

Card 2

1 Tears ran _____ her cheeks as she said goodbye to her friend.
2 Which company do you work _____?
3 He dived _____ the water.
4 I am proud _____ my country.
5 The boy jumped _____ the wall.

Card 3

1 The sun went _____ a cloud.
2 Tunbridge Wells is _____ Hastings and London.
3 Do you go to work _____ car?
4 He broke his leg when he fell _____ the stairs.
5 What did you buy your mother _____ her birthday?

Card 4

1 The children hid _____ the bed.
2 Shall I go with you _____ the station?
3 They bought a house _____ a very big garden.
4 Are you doing anything _____ the weekend?
5 She was born _____ December 10th.

Card 5

1 He comes _____ Canada.
2 There was silence when the teacher walked _____ the room.
3 The chemist's is _____ the library.
4 The door is made _____ steel.
5 Please take your feet _____ the chair.

Card 6

1 We don't go to school _____ the summer.
2 Don't look round, but the person standing _____ you is the new boss.
3 Is it expensive to travel _____ train in your country?
4 I'm looking _____ my pen. Have you seen it?
5 I got a letter _____ my cousin in Scotland today.

Card 7

1 There is a bridge _____ the river.
2 They walked home _____ the park.
3 He was wearing a vest _____ his shirt.
4 I always drive _____ work.
5 Have a biscuit _____ your coffee.

Card 8

1 She sat _____ me at the theatre.
2 He was laughing so much that he fell _____ his chair.
3 The postman pushed the letter _____ the letterbox.
4 What time do you usually go _____ school?
5 Would you like to come _____ me to the cinema tonight?

Card 9

1 My uncle talks _____ golf all the time.
2 I always have a party _____ my birthday.
3 She walked _____ the street.
4 The post office is _____ the bank and the cinema.
5 The piece of music is _____ Beethoven.

Card 10

1 Children in this country start school _____ the age of five.
2 My flat is _____ the third floor.
3 Are you interested _____ pop music?
4 'I will love you _____ ever!' he said to her.
5 I don't like stories _____ sad endings.

33 Prepositions bingo   Teacher's words

about	**across**	**at**	**behind**	**between**
by	**down**	**for**	**from**	**in**
into	**next to**	**of**	**off**	**on**
over	**through**	**under**	**to**	**with**

                    From *Grammar Games and Activities Book 1* © Penguin Books 2001

34 Two funny stories

Two old men who lived in a village deep in the country

decided one day to take a trip to London. This meant

they had to leave their village, get on a bus to the nearest

town, and there catch the train for London. It was all a big

adventure for them, as they had never done anything like it

before. To eat on the journey, they had bought some

bananas. They'd never eaten bananas before either.

They got on the train and were marvelling at the speed. One

man decided to try his banana, but just as he was taking a

bite the train entered a tunnel.

'Have you eaten your banana yet?' he called out to his
friend.

'No,' replied his friend.

'Well, don't,' said the first man. 'I took a bite of mine and
went blind.'

A motorist driving through the country stopped for a

hitch-hiker who was holding the halter of a cow.

'I can give you a lift,' he said, 'but I can't take your cow.'

'Don't worry,' said the hitch-hiker, 'she'll follow us in her own time.'

So the hitch-hiker got in and the motorist started up. He

drove at thirty miles an hour and the cow trotted along

behind him. He drove at forty miles an hour and the cow was

still trotting along behind him. He drove at fifty miles an hour

yet the cow was somehow managing to keep pace with him.

But he noticed in his mirror that the cow seemed to be tiring,

as her tongue was hanging out of her mouth. 'I'm worried

about your cow,' said the motorist to his passenger, 'her

tongue is hanging out of her mouth to the right.'

'Oh, that's all right,' said the hitch-hiker, 'that means she's

going to overtake!'

You and your partner both have an account of Andrew Scott's life but your accounts are not the same. There are 12 differences. You can ask your partner a maximum of 20 questions to find all these differences. Put a circle round what you find, but do not tell your partner!

The Life History of Andrew Scott

Andrew Scott was born in Brighton on 9th June, 1955. His father was a policeman and his mother was a tax inspector. He started school when he was five and left school when he was sixteen. In August 1972 he started work at a post office in the centre of Brighton. He stayed there for five years. Then in September 1978 he moved to London. He got a new job at a travel agency not far from Buckingham Palace.

Six months later he met Julie Parker at a party. They fell in love and got married on 26th April, 1979. Julie was an actress and when she got the chance to work in America, Andrew gave up his job and went with her. They stayed in America for eleven years altogether. During this time, Julie made ten films and was the star of a television series called *Two People*.

Andrew started writing books and in June 1982 his first book, *Brighton Sand*, was published. It sold nearly a million copies. A year later, their first child was born. They called him David after Andrew's grandfather. They had two more children while they were in America – Emily, who was born in 1985 and Simon who was born in 1987.

In March 1991 they moved back to Britain. They lived in Leeds at first, then three years ago they bought a very big house near Brighton. This is where they now live.

Questions

1 2 3 4 5 6 7 8 9 10 11 12 13 14 15 16 17 18 19 20

You and your partner both have an account of Andrew Scott's life but your accounts are not the same. There are 12 differences. You can ask your partner a maximum of 20 questions to find all these differences. Put a circle round what you find, but do not tell your partner!

The Life History of Andrew Scott

Andrew Scott was born in Brighton on 19th July, 1955. His father was a policeman and his mother was an estate agent. He started school when he was five and left school when he was sixteen. In August 1972 he started work at a bank in the centre of Brighton. He stayed there for five years. Then in September 1978 he moved to London. He got a new job at a travel agency not far from Trafalgar Square.

Six months later he met Julie Parker while he was on holiday. They fell in love and got married on 26th April, 1980. Julie was an actress and when she got the chance to work in America, Andrew gave up his job and went with her. They stayed in America for eleven years altogether. During this time, Julie made ten films and was the star of a television series called *Chicago*.

Andrew started writing books and in June 1982 his second book, *Brighton Sand*, was published. It sold over a million copies. A year later, their first child was born. They called him David after Andrew's father. They had two more children while they were in America – Emily, who was born in 1985 and Simon who was born in 1987.

In March 1991 they moved back to Britain. They lived in York at first, then two years ago they bought a very big house near Brighton. This is where they now live.

Questions

1 2 3 4 5 6 7 8 9 10 11 12 13 14 15 16 17 18 19 20

From *Grammar Games and Activities Book 1* © Penguin Books 2001

36 What do you remember?

1 the first time you went on holiday	**2** your first bicycle	**3** a relative (from the past)	**4** one of your best friends at primary school
5 a party you really enjoyed	**6** your grandparents	**7** an important event from your childhood (*first or last day at school, moving home, etc.*)	**8** your last school report
9 a teacher at school you either liked a lot or hated a lot	**10** the town or village where you grew up	**11** the first famous person you admired	**12** your bedroom when you were ten years old
13 your favourite TV programme last year	**14** the plot of the last book you read	**15** the first money you ever earned	**16** a wedding day – yours or someone else's
17 your first (*or favourite*) house/flat	**18** an experience that was either frightening or embarrassing	**19** a hobby you used to have	**20** a holiday you didn't enjoy very much

37 Are you the person I'm looking for?

Find someone: 1

1 who can ski. _____
2 who doesn't have a driving licence. _____
3 who came here today by bus. _____
4 who has appeared on TV. _____
5 who was born on the same day of the week as you were. _____

Find someone: 2

1 who can remember what the weather was like last week. _____
2 who drinks more than six cups of tea or coffee a day. _____
3 who went abroad last summer. _____
4 who has never flown. _____
5 whose father has the same name as yours. _____

Find someone: 3

1 who can dance the lambada. _____
2 who doesn't have a mobile phone. _____
3 who got up before 7 o'clock this morning. _____
4 who has been hypnotised. _____
5 who was born in the same month as you were. _____

Find someone: 4

1 who can make a funny face. _____
2 who has a computer at home. _____
3 who started school before he/she was six. _____
4 who has never smoked or drunk alcohol. _____
5 whose mother has the same name as yours. _____

Find someone: 5

1 who can do a handstand. _____
2 who doesn't have any brothers or sisters. _____
3 who went to bed late last night. _____
4 who has been to more than four schools. _____
5 who was not born in hospital. _____

Find someone: 6

1 who can whistle. _____
2 who feels faint at the sight of blood. _____
3 who can remember their dreams. _____
4 who knows what the capital of Wales is. _____
5 who has the same number of brothers and sisters as you. _____

Find someone: 7

1 who can hum the British National Anthem. _____
2 who doesn't want to get married. _____
3 who was born in a village. _____
4 who has been skiing recently. _____
5 who started school at the same age as you did. _____

Find someone: 8

1 who can't swim. _____
2 who looks forward to going to the dentist. _____
3 who hated school. _____
4 who has been to Moscow or Copenhagen. _____
5 who has the same interests as you have. _____

Find someone: 9

1 who can make a sound like a chicken. _____
2 who doesn't like watching sport. _____
3 who was born in January. _____
4 who has never been abroad. _____
5 whose favourite pop group is the same as yours. _____

Find someone: 10

1 who can read music. _____
2 who has an exciting hobby. _____
3 who didn't watch TV last night. _____
4 who has more than one best friend. _____
5 who doesn't usually read a daily newspaper. _____

Photocopiable   From *Grammar Games and Activities Book 1* © Penguin Books 2001

37 Are you the person I'm looking for?

Find someone: **11**

1 who can spell his/her name backwards. _____
2 who has relatives in Britain. _____
3 who bought a new computer. _____
4 who has worked in a restaurant _____
5 who thinks learning English is easy. _____

Find someone: **12**

1 who can speak more than two foreign languages. _____
2 who has more than four brothers and sisters. _____
3 who liked cabbage as a child. _____
4 who has never been in love. _____
5 who has a penfriend from another country. _____

Find someone: **13**

1 who can skate backwards. _____
2 whose brother or sister works in a hospital. _____
3 whose father or mother worked in a bank. _____
4 who has been learning English for more than 6 years. _____
5 who wants to be famous. _____

Find someone: **14**

1 who has ridden a motorbike. _____
2 who thinks he/she is shy. _____
3 who learnt more than one foreign language at school. _____
4 who has never eaten Chinese food. _____
5 who would know how to give the 'kiss of life'. _____

Find someone: **15**

1 who can wake up without an alarm clock. _____
2 who feels sick when people are smoking nearby. _____
3 who grew up in a large city. _____
4 who has been inside the Tower of London. _____
5 who takes the same size in shoes as you do. _____

Find someone: **16**

1 who can wink with both eyes. _____
2 who thinks he's/she's a good cook. _____
3 who used to bite his/her nails. _____
4 who has read a book by Charles Dickens. _____
5 who would like to change his/her name. _____

Find someone: **17**

1 who can understand computer manuals. _____
2 who has never flown. _____
3 who had something to eat just before this lesson. _____
4 who has made more than two speeches in public. _____
5 who thinks babies are boring. _____

Find someone: **18**

1 who can guess what your favourite colour is. _____
2 who thinks he/she is stubborn. _____
3 who saw his/her grandparents last weekend. _____
4 who has tried to lose weight. _____
5 who can raise one eyebrow. _____

Find someone: **19**

1 who can touch his/her toes. _____
2 who thinks he/she is romantic. _____
3 who walked here today. _____
4 who has moved into a new house or flat recently. _____
5 who can guess how much you weigh. _____

Find someone: **20**

1 who can say 'I love you' in more than three languages. _____
2 who is left-handed. _____
3 who can't stand soap operas. _____
4 who has spoken to or shaken hands with a famous person. _____
5 who has no time for hobbies. _____

Although he was rich . . .

As it was raining . . .

We'll go out . . .

As long as she got well paid . . .

Because she didn't have a car . . .

I wouldn't go out with her . . .

I'll give you £5 . . .

He's a marvellous painter . . .

Take a torch with you . . .

We went for a swim . . .

She'll be an excellent teacher . . .

Provided that they don't do anything stupid . . .

I couldn't lend him any money . . .

He bought a new suit . . .

It was so cold . . .

Unless he arrives soon . . .

Everyone has to die . . .

Whatever you do, James, . . .

When it rains a lot . . .

I always feel like dancing . . .

 From *Grammar Games and Activities Book 1* © Penguin Books 2001

38 Broken sentences

. . . he lived a relatively simple life.
. . . they cancelled the picnic.
. . . as soon as it stops raining.
. . . she didn't mind what she had to do.
. . . she could afford to go by taxi more often.
. . . even if you paid me.
. . . if you do me a favour.
. . . in spite of being almost blind.
. . . in case it gets dark.
. . . even though the water was freezing.
. . . once she's had a bit more experience.
. . . they should win tonight's match easily.
. . . since I was practically broke myself.
. . . so that he could make a good impression.
. . . that the lake froze.
. . . we'll have to go without him.
. . . whether they like it or not.
. . . don't upset her!
. . . my roof starts to leak.
. . . whenever I hear Salsa music.

39 Ask the right question

tennis	by boat	frightened	tomorrow
Stockholm	Spain	blue	yesterday
Margaret Thatcher	a cow	strawberries	Beethoven
a cat	vegetables	on Sunday	in June
I love you	Bad luck!	thirsty	How do you do?
milk	in 1990	last year	my father
No, thank you.	Yes, I can.	No, never.	a computer
2 weeks ago	bananas	a Fancy Dress party	the theatre
Shakespeare	nervous	angry	a newspaper
on holiday	Keep the change!	John Lennon	for sale

 From *Grammar Games and Activities Book 1* © Penguin Books 2001

40　The longest day

These are the missing verbs from the story.

became	gave	make	reached
caught	got	make sure	set out
could	had finished	met	slept
decided	had left	misread	understand
drove	hitchhiking	missed	welcomed
explained	know	persuade	were sent
found	lost	put	woke up

Gaps:

1 _____

2 _____

3 _____

4 _____

5 _____

6 _____

7 _____

8 _____

9 _____

10 _____

11 _____

12 _____

13 _____

14 _____

15 _____

16 _____

17 _____

18 _____

19 _____

20 _____

21 _____

22 _____

23 _____

24 _____

25 _____

25 _____

26 _____

27 _____

28 _____

41 Old school friends

Student A

Imagine that you and your partner were at school together and that you meet at an airport several years later. When you were friends at school:

you told him/her you were going to:	your partner told you he/she was going to:
leave home at 17 ✔ become a pop singer ✔ move to Los Angeles buy your parents a big house marry a foreigner ✔ have two children write a musical ✔ own a race horse grow your hair long ✔ have lots of money (✔ = these came true)	go to university become a doctor or pilot buy a sports car marry Mark (or Emma) Taylor have lots of children move to London work abroad learn to fly an aeroplane write a novel make a lot of money

Find out what happened to his/her plans. He/she will also ask you about yours. Be prepared to use your imagination and try to ask lots of questions about why his/her plans came true or didn't come true.

---

41 Old school friends

Student B

Imagine that you and your partner were at school together and that you meet at an airport several years later. When you were friends at school:

you told him/her you were going to:	your partner told you he/she was going to:
go to university ✔ become a doctor or pilot buy a sports car ✔ marry Mark (or Emma) Taylor have lots of children move to London ✔ work abroad ✔ learn to fly an aeroplane write a novel make a lot of money ✔ (✔ = these came true)	leave home at 17 become a pop singer move to Los Angeles buy his/her parents a big house marry a foreigner have two children write a musical own a race horse grow his/her hair long have lots of money

Find out what happened to his/her plans. He/she will also ask you about yours. Be prepared to use your imagination and try to ask lots of questions about why his/her plans came true or didn't come true.

Photocopiable From *Grammar Games and Activities Book 1* © Penguin Books 2001

window

window

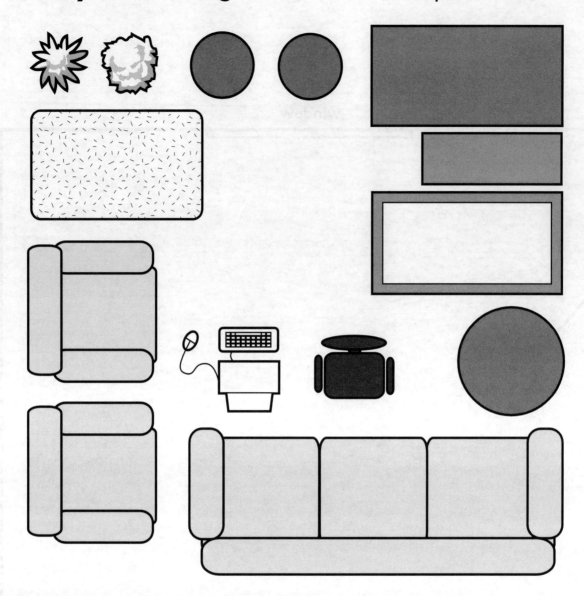

42 My ideal living room

Key

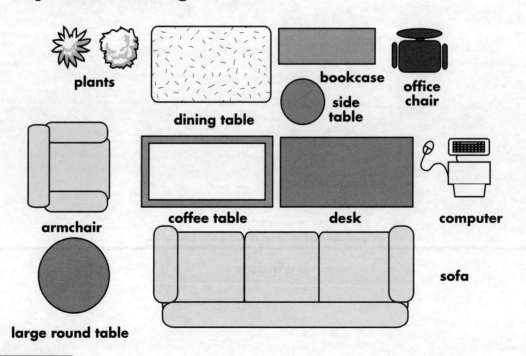

plants

dining table

bookcase

side table

office chair

armchair

coffee table

desk

computer

large round table

sofa

From *Grammar Games and Activities Book 1* © Penguin Books 2001

42 My ideal living room

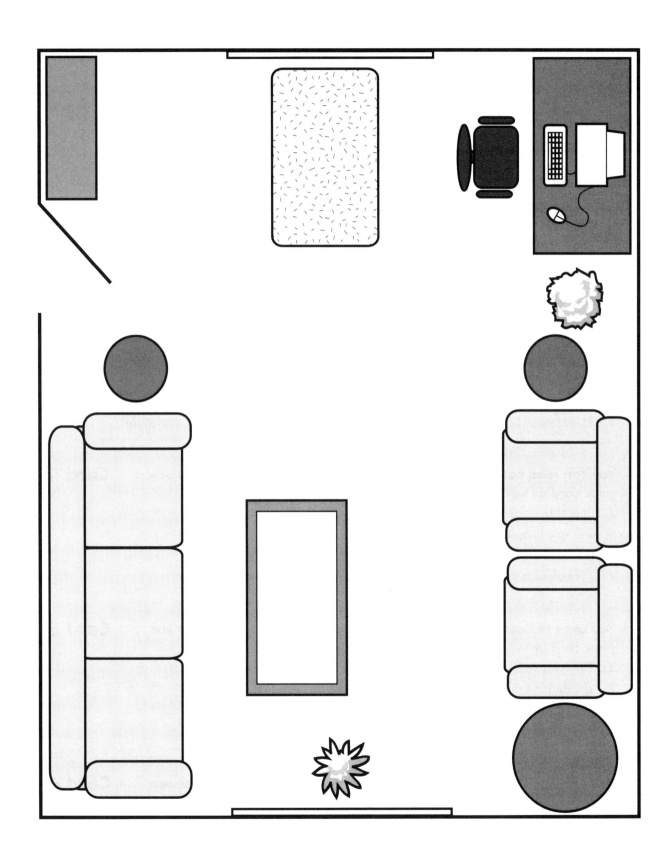

 107

42 My ideal living room

You can read out the following, but you must not let anyone else see your card or write anything down. **Card 1**
1 The bookcase is behind the door.
2 The dining table is in front of the window.
3 The desk is in the corner, opposite the door.
4 The sofa is in the corner.

You can read out the following, but you must not let anyone else see your card or write anything down. **Card 2**
1 The bookcase is against the wall, facing the dining table.
2 The side tables are opposite each other.
3 The coffee table is in front of the sofa.
4 The two armchairs are next to the large round table.

You can read out the following, but you must not let anyone else see your card or write anything down. **Card 3**
1 The long side of the dining table is parallel to the door.
2 The office chair is in front of the desk.
3 There is a plant between one of the side tables and the desk.
4 As you open the door to leave the room, the bookcase is facing you on your right.

You can read out the following, but you must not let anyone else see your card or write anything down. **Card 4**
1 One of the side tables is next to the sofa, near the door.
2 The sofa is opposite the armchairs.
3 As you enter the room, the large round table is in the right-hand corner.
4 The sofa is not against any of the walls with windows.

You can read out the following, but you must not let anyone else see your card or write anything down. **Card 5**
1 The computer is on the desk.
2 The dining table is near the door.
3 One of the plants is in the middle of one of the windows.
4 The two armchairs are next to each other.

You can read out the following, but you must not let anyone else see your card or write anything down. **Card 6**
1 As you enter the room, the sofa is immediately on your right.
2 One of the side tables is next to one of the armchairs.
3 There is a plant between the sofa and the large round table.
4 The armchairs are against the wall opposite the door.

   From *Grammar Games and Activities Book 1* © Penguin Books 2001

43 Trivia search

You know the following: 1

- When a gorilla is angry it will stick its tongue out at you.
- Dolphins sleep with one eye open all the time.
- Chewing gum while peeling onions will keep you from crying.

You want to know:

1 which the first country to elect a female Member of Parliament was.
2 how to tell if a person is right-handed or left-handed.
3 what is different about telephone directories in Iceland.

You know the following: 2

- In Tibet, when guests arrive at your house you greet them by sticking your tongue out at them.
- The average new-born baby spends 113 minutes a day crying.
- The great Greek writer Aeschylus is said to have been killed when an eagle dropped a tortoise on his head.

You want to know:

1 when and where the first driving licences were made compulsory.
2 what a gorilla does when it is angry.
3 which creature can crawl over a razor blade without cutting itself.

You know the following: 3

- You can find out whether a mosquito is male or female by letting it land on you. If it bites you, it's female.
- It is not unusual to see a woman smoking a cigar in Denmark.
- Just before you are struck by lightning, all the hair on your head will stand on end.

You want to know:

1 how long a new-born baby spends crying every day.
2 an unusual way of finding out an elephant's approximate height.
3 how long a python can live without food.

You know the following: 4

- A python can go for as long as a year without eating.
- In ancient Greece a woman's age was counted from the first day of her marriage.
- Finland was the first country to have a female Member of Parliament in 1907, when nine women were voted in.

You want to know:

1 how to find out whether a mosquito is male or female.
2 a way to stop you crying when peeling onions.
3 how the famous Greek writer Aeschylus was killed.

You know the following: 5

- People in Iceland are listed in the telephone directories by their first names, not their surnames.
- The first driving licences were made compulsory in Paris in 1893.
- The flag of Italy was designed by Napoleon Bonaparte.

You want to know:

1 why in ancient Greece it was very difficult to know how old a woman really was.
2 what happens to you just before you are struck by lightning.
3 how dolphins usually sleep.

You know the following: 6

- If you measure the distance around an elephant's foot and double it, you will find out its approximate height.
- A snail can crawl over a razor blade without cutting itself.
- You can generally tell if a person is right-handed or left-handed by which foot they put into their trousers first.

You want to know:

1 how people in Tibet usually greet guests.
2 who designed the flag of Italy.
3 what a fairly common sight in Denmark is.

44 Find the other half

He was delighted . . .	. . . with his present.
She was worried . . .	. . . about the exam.
She was always kind . . .	. . . to animals.
He was rude . . .	. . . to his grandmother.
He was fed up . . .	. . . with the bad weather.
We were shocked . . .	. . . at the news.
She wasn't satisfied . . .	. . . with her exam results.
He is afraid . . .	. . . of spiders and snakes.
She was ashamed . . .	. . . of her parents.
We are proud . . .	. . . of our country.
He was jealous . . .	. . . of my success.
I was suspicious . . .	. . . of his intentions.

Photocopiable

44 Find the other half

I'm not very good . . .	. . . at maths.
My sister is married . . .	. . . to an Australian.
He was sorry . . .	. . . for his bad behaviour.
This country is famous . . .	. . . for its lakes.
She is responsible . . .	. . . for the mess.
I'm very interested . . .	. . . in tennis.
She's very fond . . .	. . . of children.
They were tired . . .	. . . of waiting.
Your dress is similar . . .	. . . to mine.
Your answer is different . . .	. . . from mine.
The room was crowded . . .	. . . with people.
I can't pay. I'm short . . .	. . . of money.

45 What sort of person are you?

Fill in column 1 on the card below about yourself, then interview five other people in the class. Only tick (✔) the box if they answer YES. (You will also be asked questions.)

Which of these statements apply to you?	1	2	3	4	5	6
I always like to keep my things neat and tidy.						
I am a good listener.						
I am a hard worker.						
I am easily influenced by friends.						
I am usually willing to compromise and cooperate.						
I am good with my hands.						
I am not particularly interested in money.						
I can forget my problems very easily.						
I am musical.						
I enjoy being on my own.						
I find it difficult to admit that I may be wrong.						
I am honest.						

1

Fill in column 1 on the card below about yourself, then interview five other people in the class. Only tick (✔) the box if they answer YES. (You will also be asked questions.)

Which of these statements apply to you?	1	2	3	4	5	6
I am ambitious.						
I am usually calm and not easily upset.						
I am fashion-conscious.						
I am often afraid that I may look ridiculous or make a fool of myself.						
I am satisfied with my appearance.						
I am superstitious.						
I enjoy eating good food.						
I can relax quite easily.						
I enjoy being the centre of attention.						
I find it hard to talk to strangers.						
I find that my first impression of a person is usually correct.						
I get upset if someone criticizes me.						

2

 From *Grammar Games and Activities Book 1* © Penguin Books 2001

45 What sort of person are you?

Fill in column 1 on the card below about yourself, then interview five other people in the class. Only tick (✔) the box if they answer YES. (You will also be asked questions.)

Which of these statements apply to you?	1	2	3	4	5	6
I am concerned about my appearance.						
I am essentially very cautious, conventional and conservative.						
I am impulsive.						
I am sure of myself.						
I am very attached to my family and friends.						
I am very good at hiding my true feelings.						
I feel anxious when I speak in front of a large group.						
I find it difficult to say no.						
I have a tendency to give up easily when I meet a difficult problem.						
I love a challenge and function best under stress.						
On the whole I am a very optimistic person.						
I often help other people.						

3

Fill in column 1 on the card below about yourself, then interview five other people in the class. Only tick (✔) the box if they answer YES. (You will also be asked questions.)

Which of these statements apply to you?	1	2	3	4	5	6
I am interested in the latest fashion.						
I am optimistic.						
I am very faithful to my friends and always keep promises.						
I am very practical by nature.						
I feel embarrassed when looking at photographs of myself.						
I frequently suffer from insomnia.						
I get upset if things don't go according to plan.						
I like to share my problems with my friends.						
I often worry that I will do or say the wrong thing.						
I prefer to be at home rather than go to parties.						
I work best in a team.						
I am self-confident.						

4

45 What sort of person are you?

Fill in column 1 on the card below about yourself, then interview five other people in the class. Only tick (✔) the box if they answer YES. (You will also be asked questions.)

Which of these statements apply to you?	1	2	3	4	5	6
I am shy and self-conscious in social situations.						
I am very careful about the way I dress.						
I am warm-hearted and usually generous to others.						
I care very much if people like me or not.						
I get embarrassed very easily.						
I frequently suffer from insomnia.						
I like to work by myself in my own way.						
I love luxury, beauty and pleasure.						
I often think 'I wish I were a child again.'						
I prefer eating good food in style rather than grabbing a quick meal.						
I prefer to listen than to talk.						
I sometimes have difficulty controlling my temper.						

5

Fill in column 1 on the card below about yourself, then interview five other people in the class. Only tick (✔) the box if they answer YES. (You will also be asked questions.)

Which of these statements apply to you?	1	2	3	4	5	6
One of my main aims in life is to do something that will make my parents proud of me.						
Once I have made my mind up I seldom change it.						
I prefer to stay in the background rather than push myself forward.						
I tend to be very lucky.						
It's difficult to find anything to talk about when I meet a new person.						
Large groups of people make me nervous.						
I get easily upset by things.						
I usually end up making the decisions when I am with a group.						
I love nothing better than a challenge.						
I try to get my own way.						
I don't really worry about what others think of me.						
I sometimes have difficulty controlling my temper.						

6

   From *Grammar Games and Activities Book 1* © Penguin Books 2001

46 Strange but true

Work with a partner. Ask and answer questions to find the missing information in the following extracts from a book of amazing facts.

Before you start, work out which questions to ask, e.g.,

What happened to Queen Elizabeth of England at an early age?

Where does Indian ink actually come from?

Why did the Germans used to keep frogs as live barometers?

1 Elephants cannot jump.

2 Queen Elizabeth I of England _____ at an early age.

3 Until 1957 it was illegal to _____ in Wales on a Sunday.

4 _____ were first developed to help the blind.

5 For the first six or seven months of our lives, we can do something that we are never able to do again; swallow and breathe at the same time.

6 In order to be the last name in the local telephone directory, a Chicago man changed his name to Zeke Zzzypt.

7 Sir Winston Churchill was a well-known Shakespearean actor before he became a politician.

8 The yo-yo was originally a Filipino jungle weapon.

9 Goldfish will often turn white if _____.

10 When Ian Fleming wrote his first James Bond book, his 007 hero was called _____.

11 King Louis XIV of France was the first person, male or female, to wear high heels.

12 The Germans used to keep frogs as live barometers because they _____.

13 Indian ink actually comes from _____.

14 To conserve metal, the _____ during World War II were made of wood.

15 The word 'tip' is an abbreviation of '_____'.

16 _____ was invented by the Chinese nearly 2,000 years ago.

17 It is impossible to sneeze and keep your eyes open at the same time.

18 Bumping foreheads with a handshake is the traditional greeting in Tibet.

19 The corkscrew was first invented to pull out teeth.

20 When George I came to the throne of England he could not speak a word of English.

46 Strange but true

Work with a partner. Ask and answer questions to find the missing information in the following extracts from a book of amazing facts.

Before you start, work out which questions to ask, e.g.,

What was the yo-yo originally?
What can't elephants do?
Where/In which country is bumping foreheads with a handshake the traditional greeting?

1 Elephants cannot _____.

2 Queen Elizabeth I of England went completely bald at an early age.

3 Until 1957 it was illegal to go swimming in Wales on a Sunday.

4 Typewriters were first developed to help the blind.

5 For the first six or seven months of our lives, we can do something we are never able to do again; _____.

6 In order to be the last name in the local telephone directory, a Chicago man changed his name to _____.

7 Sir Winston Churchill was a _____ before he became a politician.

8 The yo-yo was originally _____.

9 Goldfish will often turn white if left in a darkened room.

10 When Ian Fleming wrote his first James Bond book, his 007 hero was called Rupert de Vere.

11 King Louis XIV of France was the first person, male or female, to wear _____.

12 The Germans used to keep frogs as live barometers because they croak when the pressure drops.

13 Indian ink actually comes from China.

14 To conserve metal, the Oscars given out at the Academy Awards during World War II were made of wood.

15 The word 'tip' is an abbreviation of 'To Insure Promptness'.

16 A form of golf was invented by the Chinese nearly 2,000 years ago.

17 It is impossible to _____ at the same time.

18 Bumping foreheads with a handshake is the traditional greeting in _____.

19 The corkscrew was first invented to _____.

20 When George I came to the throne of England he could not _____.

 From *Grammar Games and Activities Book 1* © Penguin Books 2001

47 Have you ever ...?

Work in groups of 5–8. Think of the people in the group then, working alone guess how many of them have done the various things. Check to see how accurate you were by asking each other questions. Finally, fill in the missing words in the sentences below. Choose from the following:

1 All of us/Everyone	**3** Some of us	**5** Hardly any of us
2 Most of us	**4** Only a few of us	**6** None of us/No one

		How many?	Correct?
1 _____ has/have been in hospital.		☐	☐
2 _____ has/have visited a Scandinavian country.		☐	☐
3 _____ has/have been seasick.		☐	☐
4 _____ has/have been to the USA.		☐	☐
5 _____ has/have been to a circus.		☐	☐
6 _____ has/have had our name in a newspaper.		☐	☐
7 _____ has/have stayed up the whole night.		☐	☐
8 _____ has/have eaten goat's cheese.		☐	☐
9 _____ has/have had a penfriend.		☐	☐
10 _____ has/have acted in a play or sung in a musical.		☐	☐
11 _____ has/have spoken to someone from Wales or Scotland.		☐	☐
12 _____ has/have sung karaoke.		☐	☐
13 _____ has/have dreamed about something that actually happened later.		☐	☐
14 _____ has/have failed a test or an exam.		☐	☐
15 _____ has/have saved somebody's life.		☐	☐
16 _____ has/have met a famous person.		☐	☐
17 _____ has/have been terrified by a book or film.		☐	☐
18 _____ has/have won money in a raffle or competition.		☐	☐
19 _____ has/have tried to smuggle something through Customs after a holiday.		☐	☐
20 _____ has/have made a speech in public.		☐	☐

Read through the following sentences and write your answers in the diagram below. Be sure to number your answers 1–12. Write down:

1 the first name of the person who influenced you most when you were a child.

2 the name of the town or village where you were born.

3 the name of the subject you hated most at school.

4 your favourite possession (e.g. a car, a watch, a computer, etc.)

5 the name of the job you would like to have if you could choose any job in the world.

6 the surname of someone (*still alive*) you don't like very much.

7 two things you really enjoy doing.

8 the year when you first went abroad. If you have never been abroad, the year you first went away on holiday.

9 the name of the most beautiful area in your country.

10 the year in which something really important happened to you.

11 the number of years you have had your present job. If you are unemployed, how long you have been out of work. If you are still studying, write down the year you think you will start work.

12 two things that worry you.

Now show your partner your diagram, but don't let him/her see your questions. See if your partner can guess what your answers refer to and give some details. Also ask your partner questions about what he/she has written. Try to make your partner talk as much as possible!

All about me

   From *Grammar Games and Activities Book 1* © Penguin Books 2001

48 Getting to know you

Read through the following sentences and write your answers in the diagram below. Be sure to number your answers 1–12. Write down:

1 the number of years you have lived in your present town or village.

2 the first name of someone you really disliked at school.

3 the name of the town or country where you had the nicest holiday you can remember.

4 two things you hate doing (e.g. ironing, homework, etc.).

5 the name of the subject you were worst at when you were at school.

6 the surname of your favourite relative.

7 what your present job is. If you are unemployed, what your last job was. If you are still studying, the job you hope to get.

8 the number of people there are in your family. Include parents, grandparents, brothers, sisters, own children.

9 a date where something really important happened to you.

10 anything you are afraid of (e.g. spiders, death, etc.).

11 the name of the country you would like to go to if you ever decided to emigrate.

12 the full name of the person (*living or dead*) you admire most.

Now show your partner your diagram, but don't let him/her see your questions. See if your partner can guess what your answers refer to and give some details. Also ask your partner questions about what he/she has written. Try to make your partner talk as much as possible!

All about me

49 House share   Student A

You have been sharing a large house with two other people for nearly two years. One of them has now decided to leave so you have to find someone to take his/her place. You have put the above advertisement in the local newspaper. Someone (your partner) phones you up about it.

Before you start, think about the following:

- where the house is situated
- when the person can move in
- how much the rent is
- how much of the house is shared
- who does the cleaning, etc.
- anything else you can think of (e.g. near the shops, station, modern, central heating, etc.)

THIRD PERSON required to share large house. Own room – share kitchen, bathroom, sitting room and garden. Central. Close station. Phone 2356-4567 after 6 pm or weekends

If the person is interested, arrange a day and time when he/she can come and see the house.

---

49 House share   Student B

You have just moved to this town and are looking for a house or flat to rent. You see the above advertisement and decide to phone up about it. Your partner answers the phone.

Before you start, think of some questions to ask. For example, you might want to know:

- where it is
- when you can move in
- how much the rent is
- what the other people are like
- how much of the house is shared
- if everyone helps with the cleaning, cooking, etc.
- what 'your room' is like
- if it is near a supermarket, etc.

THIRD PERSON required to share large house. Own room – share kitchen, bathroom, sitting room and garden. Central. Close station. Phone 2356-4567 after 6 pm or weekends

If the person is interested, try to arrange a day and time to go and see it. You can start by saying:

Good (morning). I'm phoning about your advertisement in the paper.

           From Grammar Games and Activities Book 1 © Penguin Books 2001

50 Hot issues

Disagree   **Agree**

Q	1	2	3	4	5	6	7	8	9	10
1										
2										
3										
4										
5										
6										
7										
8										
9										
10										
11										
12										
13										
14										
15										

51 Taking a group photograph
Photo 1

Imagine you are a photographer. Arrange the five people in your group so that they look like the following drawing:

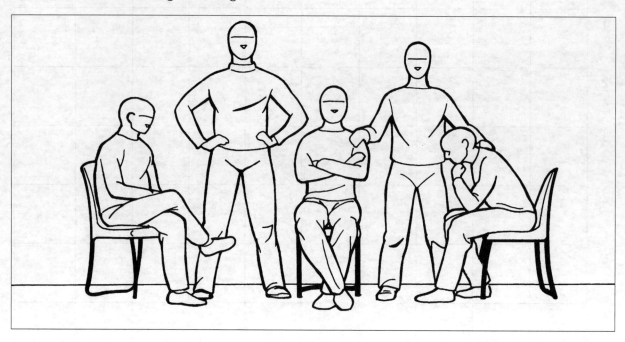

When you have finished, ask your teacher to give you a mark out of ten for your 'photograph'.

---

51 Taking a group photograph
Photo 2

Imagine you are a photographer. Arrange the five people in your group so that they look like the following drawing:

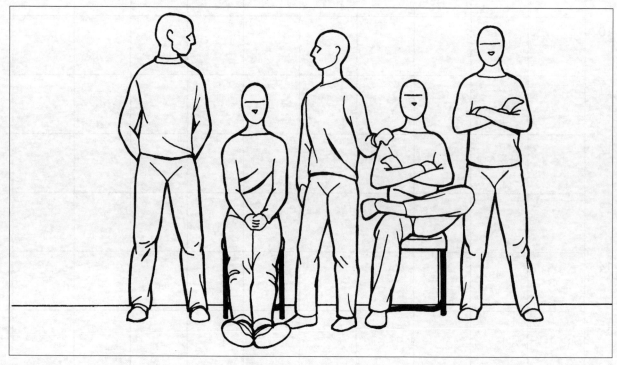

When you have finished, ask your teacher to give you a mark out of ten for your 'photograph'.

52 Reasons and excuses

Read out the following to your partner.

Write your answers here.

1 Number 1. You've put on weight.

2 Number 2. The window's broken!

3 Number 3. Carol looks happy.

4 Number 4. Peter's in a really bad mood today.

5 Number 5. You forgot to phone me!

6 Number 6. Pam and Dave aren't talking to each other.

7 _____

8 _____

9 _____

10 _____

11 _____

12 _____

---

52 Reasons and excuses

Write your answers here.

1 _____

2 _____

3 _____

4 _____

5 _____

6 _____

Read out the following to your partner.

7 Number 7. Your hands are dirty!

8 Number 8. It's freezing in here!

9 Number 9. You still haven't paid me back the £20 you owe me!

10 Number 10. My car won't start.

11 Number 11. You're late again!

12 Number 12. Janet's lost her voice.

53 Countable or uncountable?

COUNTABLE	UNCOUNTABLE
advance	advice
animal	behaviour
briefcase	equipment
brochure	excitement
camera	furniture
city	health
coin	homework
competition	information
exercise	knowledge
family	luggage
flight	news
flower	permission
impression	progress
job	research
key	scenery
newspaper	traffic
opinion	training
sofa	travel
suggestion	weather
war	work

Photocopiable   From *Grammar Games and Activities Book 1* © Penguin Books 2001

54 What a question!

For a person you loved deeply, would you be willing to move to a distant country knowing there would be little chance of ever seeing your family and friends again?	If you knew there would be a nuclear war in one week, what would you do?	**Would you have one of your fingers surgically removed if it somehow guaranteed immunity from all major diseases?**	You discover your wonderful 2-year-old daughter is, because of a mix-up at the hospital, not yours. Would you want to exchange the child to try to correct the mistake?
Would you accept twenty-five years of extraordinary happiness if it meant you would die at the end of the period?	Would you accept a job twice as good as your present one – twice as much money and twice as fulfilling – given one condition of employment; you can never reveal anything about it to anyone you know?	You are given the power to kill people. They would die a natural death and no one would suspect you. Are there any situations in which you would use this power?	Your house, containing everything you own, catches fire. After saving your loved ones and pets, you have time to safely make a final dash to save any one item. What would it be?
If you were having difficulty in an important test and could safely cheat by looking at someone else's paper, would you do so?	Would you rather be extremely successful professionally and have a fairly ordinary private life, or have a very happy private life and only an ordinary professional life?	In front of you are ten pistols – only one of which is loaded. For £1 million would you pick one up, point it at your head and press the trigger? If you survive, you keep the money.	If you could take a one-month trip anywhere in the world and money were not a consideration, where would you go and what would you do?
If you could script the basic plot for the dream you will have tonight, what would the story be?	Would you be willing to become extremely ugly physically if it meant you would live for 500 years at any physical age you chose?	Would you be willing to reduce your life expectancy by five years to become extremely attractive?	Assuming that you had no children and felt the only way to have a family was to marry someone you didn't love, would you be willing to do so?
Would you be willing to murder an innocent person if it would end hunger in the world?	For £20,000 would you go for three months without washing, brushing your teeth, or using a deodorant? Assume you could not explain your reasons to anyone.	Given the ability to project yourself into the past but not return, would you do so? Where would you go and what would you try to accomplish if you knew you might change the course of history?	If a crystal ball would tell you the truth about any one thing you wished to know concerning yourself, life, the future, or anything else, what would you want to know?

36 ask	37 ask	38 tell	39 ask	40 tell	41 tell	42 ask	End
35 tell							
34 ask	33 tell	32 ask	31 tell	30 tell	29 ask	28 tell	27 ask
							26 tell
18 tell	19 ask	20 tell	21 tell	22 tell	23 ask	24 tell	25 ask
17 ask							
16 ask	15 ask	14 tell	13 ask	12 tell	11 ask	10 tell	9 tell
							8 ask
Start	1 ask	2 tell	3 ask	4 tell	5 ask	6 ask	7 tell

From *Grammar Games and Activities Book 1* © Penguin Books 2001

ask cards	**Ask someone:** why he/she wants to learn English.	**Ask someone:** what sort of things he/she is afraid of.	**Ask someone:** which person from history he/she hates most.	**Ask someone:** if there is something he/she would like to buy one day.	**Ask someone:** what sort of things make him/her happy.
Ask someone: to say something about the main political parties in his/her country.	**Ask someone:** what he/she usually does in the evenings.	**Ask someone:** what sort of things make him/her laugh.	**Ask someone:** to tell you about a dream he/she remembers.	**Ask someone:** about any pets he/she has (or used to have).	**Ask someone:** to tell you about the most exciting thing that has ever happened to him/her.
Ask someone: about his/her favourite country for a holiday (and why).	**Ask someone:** if he/she is like his/her mother or father.	**Ask someone:** to tell you about the last book he/she read.	**Ask someone:** about his/her idea of the perfect teacher, husband or wife.	**Ask someone:** how he/she usually spends his/her free time.	**Ask someone:** about the place where he/she lives.
Ask someone: where he/she was born and what he/she remembers most from his/her childhood.	**Ask someone:** to describe his/her living-room.	**Ask someone:** how many new English words he/she hopes to learn on this course.	**Ask someone:** about his/her favourite sport.	**Ask someone:** to tell you two or three things he/she is not very good at.	**Ask someone:** what thing about himself/herself he/she would like to change.
Ask someone: what he/she is going to do at the weekend.	**Ask someone:** about his/her favourite restaurant.	**Ask someone:** what he/she remembers about his/her first or last day at school.	**Ask someone:** if he/she has ever been in a situation that was dangerous or frightening.	**Ask someone:** about his/her plans for the summer.	**Ask someone:** which person from history he/she would most like to have met (and why).
Ask someone: what he/she thinks is the ideal age to get married.	**Ask someone:** about the type of job he/she would like to have.	**Ask someone:** about a country he/she would like to visit (and why).	**Ask someone:** to describe a good TV programme he/she has seen recently.	**Ask someone:** what sort of films he/she likes watching.	**Ask someone:** his/her idea of a well-dressed man and woman.

tell cards	Tell the others: about someone you were really friendly with at school.	Tell the others: something about the town or village where you were born.	Tell the others: anything you can remember about the first boy/girl you were attracted to.	Tell the others: about some of the things that make you angry or annoyed.	Tell the others: why your country would be a good place to visit as a tourist.
Tell the others: about the types of clothes you like and don't like wearing.	Tell the others: something about the flat/house where you live.	Tell the others: about your last visit abroad.	Tell the others: about any other places you have lived.	Tell the others: one or two things you are quite good at.	Tell the others: which person (still alive!) you would most like to meet and why.
Tell the others: about the nicest present you have ever received.	Tell the others: something about your favourite relative.	Tell the others: about the type of music you like and dislike.	Tell the others: where you hope to go on holiday in the summer.	Tell the others: about a teacher at school you looked up to.	Tell the others: about your childhood.
Tell the others: what you like doing in your free time.	Tell the others: about any incident that made you feel embarrassed or ashamed.	Tell the others: about the type of men/women you are attracted to.	Tell the others: about a country you would not like to visit and why.	Tell the others: something about one of your brothers, sisters or friends.	Tell the others: about a good film you have seen recently.
Tell the others: about a book you would recommend that they all read.	Tell the others: where you usually go to buy clothes.	Tell the others: about someone who has made a big impression on you.	Tell the others: what things you find difficult to learn in English.	Tell the others: what things from your country you would miss if you ever emigrated.	Tell the others: about your favourite dish (and how to cook it!)
Tell the others: where you used to go and what you used to do when you were a teenager.	Tell the others: two good points and two bad points about yourself.	Tell the others: what you are planning to do after this lesson.	Tell the others: where you spent last weekend.	Tell the others: which jobs you think carry the most prestige in your country.	Tell the others: a good way of learning new words in English.

From *Grammar Games and Activities Book 1* © Penguin Books 2001

56 Keep talking!

I'm never going to speak to (him/her) again!	I'm moving next week.	I saw (him/her) again this morning.
I'm in love!	I don't know what to do about it.	That's the last time I ever do that!
I wish they would move!	I wish I hadn't told (him/her) now!	I had a really great time last night.
I've decided to quit my job.	I'm ever so worried!	I can't stand my new (boss/teacher)!

57 What does it mean?

Listen and write the numbers 1–16 next to the correct sentences.

a 'Don't let on!' _____

b 'He's always looked down on foreigners.' _____

c 'I can put you up.' _____

d 'I really must cut down.' _____

e 'I think it's going to clear up.' _____

f 'I'll call on you tonight.' _____

g 'I'm getting on a bit now.' _____

h 'I'm worn out.' _____

i 'I've been beaten up.' _____

j 'It keeps breaking down.' _____

k 'It's been held up.' _____

l 'She's passed out.' _____

m 'They've decided to take me on.' _____

n 'We had to have him put down.' _____

o 'We turn out about a thousand a day.' _____

p 'We've fallen out again.' _____

      From *Grammar Games and Activities Book 1* © Penguin Books 2001

58 Finish the sentence

The saddest thing I ever saw ...	If I only had three months left to live ...	I wish my parents were less ... and more ...	I still haven't ...
My *(brother, mother, etc.)* gets angry if ...	Two things that really give me pleasure are ... and ...	Right now I'd like to ...	I feel happiest when ...
Parents should never ...	I hate people who ...	In the next five years I'm going to ...	If I could foretell the future, I'd ...
If I were an animal, I'd like to be a/an ... because ...	The thing that worries me most about the world today ...	The one place I'd really like to visit ...	I wish teachers would ...
This country would be a better place to live in if ...	If I won £1 million, I'd ...	People should try to ...	I hardly ever ...

59 Explain yourself!

You were climbing through your neighbour's upstairs window.
You took your cousin's dog for a walk and came back with a completely different one.
You were running through the park dressed as a gorilla.
You were driving your car on the wrong side of the road.
You were chasing a policeman down the street.
You were sitting on the roof of the school crying.
You came to school with your face and arms painted blue.
You were at a disco dressed as a member of the opposite sex.
You were washing your clothes in the local river.
You were throwing stones angrily at a large Coca-Cola sign.
You were in your neighbour's house, looking through his drawers.
You were standing outside the cinema singing loudly.
You suddenly stood up after five minutes of your English exam and walked slowly out of the room.

 From *Grammar Games and Activities Book 1* © Penguin Books 2001

60 Urban myths

The following facts are all completely untrue, but are often thought to be true or have appeared in newspapers as true stories. They are known as urban myths. Read through them for five minutes. You are not allowed to write anything down.

- If a large vicious dog attacks you, the best way to avoid being badly bitten is to grab its front legs and quickly pull them apart sideways, killing the dog instantly.

- If you pick a hamster up by the tail, its eyes drop out.

- A woman once lost her watch on a Devon beach. Years later, her husband caught a fish in the same spot and it had her watch inside – still keeping perfect time.

- Scientists have invented a car that runs on water, but all the world's oil companies have got together, paid off the scientists involved, and are keeping the invention secret.

- It is quite common for dead passengers to travel around undisturbed for days on the Tokyo metro – even sometimes standing up.

- The Bank of England has to buy every new model of photocopier, fax or laser printer to see how well they can forge notes.

- You can fully recharge phone cards but putting them in the freezer overnight.

- The ink for US dollar bills comes from crushed butterfly wings.

- An ancient British law, still valid but little used, states that if you stop someone in the street and can correctly guess how much money they have in their pocket, you can keep it.

- Shop mirrors are trick ones that make you look slimmer.

- There's a special number you can dial on your telephone that will make all your calls free from then on. When people are caught doing it, they're charged with another crime and it's all hushed up.

- Dozens of commuters on London Underground kill themselves every year by falling asleep. Apparently, they wake up confused and accidentally walk out of the train door between stations.

When your teacher tells you to stop, turn your paper over. You are now going to be tested. Write your answers on a separate piece of paper. Number them 1–12.

Index to structures used

The numbers indicate the activities in which the structures are practised.

PENGUIN ENGLISH PHOTOCOPIABLES

0 582 42785 1

0 582 42784 3

0 582 46563 X

0 582 46564 8

0 582 46158 8

0 14 081562 7

0 582 42783 5

0 582 45146 9

0 582 45145 0

0 582 46901 5

0 14 081632 1

0 14 081656 9

0 582 44774 7

0 14 081619 4

0 582 42788 6

0 582 46566 4

0 582 46565 6

0 14 081680 1

0 14 081659 3

0 14 081662 3

 www.penguinenglish.com